Re-Membering Purpose

Ife Afriye Kilimanjaro, Ph.D.

Copyright 2023 by Ife Kilimanjaro

All rights reserved. No part of this book may be reproduced in any part or by any means—graphic, electronic, or mechanical—without the prior written permission of the copyright owner, except for the use of brief quotations in critical articles and reviews.

To request permissions, contact the copyright holder at info@medewnefer.com.

The material in this book is intended for education and is not intended to replace any advice by a qualified mental health professional. If the reader or anyone they know is feeling suicidal, thinking about hurting themselves or is concerned that someone they know may be in danger of hurting themselves, call 988.

Paperback: 979-8-9875352-0-2
Ebook: 979-8-9875352-1-9

Library of Congress Control Number: 2022924056

First paperback edition: January 2023

Edited by Sheree L. Greer
Cover art by Nia Kilimanjaro
Layout by Ife Kilimanjaro

Publisher
Medew Nefer
Chesterfield, VA
www.medewnefer.com

Table of Contents

Dedication	5
Gratitude	7
Foreword	9
Chapter One: Introduction	13
Reflection Space	25
Chapter Two: A Letter to Reader, My Kindred Spirit	27
Chapter Three: Conversations With My Soul	29
Reflection Space	73
Chapter Four: A Letter to Reader, My Kindred Spirit	75
Reflection Space	83
Chapter Five: Conversations With My Ancestors	85
Reflection Space	141
Chapter Six: Conversations With The Mothers Earth and Their Children	143
Reflection Space	167
Chapter Seven: My Gift to Reader, My Kindred Spirit	169
Reflection Space	185
Afterword	187
Resources for Support	191

Dedication

To my ancestors and spirit guides
To my teachers and mentors
To my loved ones, blood and chosen
To my relatives of all forms
To those yet to come
This is for you

Nia, it is you that inspired me to put pen to paper and write this book. This is for you.

Mom, you who have given me life, who made the decision to allow me to grow inside your young womb, it is because of you that i can make this journey in the first place. This is for you.

Granddaughter, this is for you.

phoenix rising from ashes
each new emergence resoundingly joyful
robust in its glory
bursting with love and light
spreading hummus rich Black nutrient-full
across the lands and
in the people
learn dear one learn
and grow and do and change the world as
you've come
to do
feed forever with your gifts
and bring them again

Seekers of Truth, Defenders of Justice, Light Bringers, Healers, Revolutionaries, and Freedom Fighters, this is for you.

Gratitude

My ancestors and spirit guides.

My mom, aunts, and spiritual mothers.

My teacher Nana Ankobiahene Oparebea Bekoe.

My sister with whom i was raised and who has taught me so much.

My newly discovered sisters whom are showing me things i had been unwilling to see.

My daughters Nia, Tdjiri, Bianca, and Lakyrra.

My grand Phoe.

My life partner.

The Wind & The Warrior: Nana Korantema, Nana Fofie, Karma Mayet.

My spiritual communities: The Circle of Light Society and Ile Ominira Ilu.

My writing accountability group: Dara Cooper, Dr. Monica White, Rev. Dr. Heber Brown.

My editor and writing coach: Sheree L. Greer.

Readers and contributors: adrienne maree brown, Dr. Monica White, Dr. Alexis Pauline Gumbs, Jacqueline Calhoun, Lorna Fleming, Jacqui Patterson, Abby Terris, Shaundale Rénā, Nia Kilimanjaro, Sarah Hodgdon.

Kin: Tdka Maat Kilimanjaro.

KickStarter Supporters.

Foreword

There we were, in a Magnolia, Mississippi front yard that a black woman millionaire had bought and transformed into a meditation center. And the priests were at work. Ife Afriye Kilimanjaro, Karma Mayet, Nana Korantema and Nana Fofie were washing us in flowers.

During this, one of the closing moments of The Wind & The Warrior retreat, I fell out of time and space. A few months earlier I had decided to attend this exciting retreat at the intersection of creativity, spirituality, and social change. I admired the brilliance and vision of the 4 co-organizers, other beloved friends and collaborators were going, and I love the Flowering Lotus meditation center. So, I decided to show up. I had no idea that I was going to end up in the midst of a ceremony where these same sisters, who I didn't even know were Akan priests, would be anointing me with flowers, speaking sacred Akan words and activating healing for a whole segment of my lineage that was waiting to embrace me.

I still don't have the words to describe what it meant for me, descendent of an Ashanti woman named Boda who survived the middle passage and rebirthed us all in the Caribbean, to sit and receive the sacred medicine of prayer in the exact language that my ancestors needed to hear it in. Could this have been one of Boda's prayers? That though she was ripped away from her community and the sacred practices that had held her ancestors for thousands of years, one day at least one of her descendants would be cleansed in a way she could recognize?

All I know is that when Ife Afriye reached out to ask me to write this preface, it was Boda who said yes. Immediately. Before I had even read the book. May the miracles in my life never ever be limited by what I know or don't know. The universe always has something better for me than I can imagine. And the universe is blessing you right now through this book.

Now that I have read *Re-Membering Purpose* I am rejoicing for YOU, because you get to experience Ife Afriye's portal making magic. It will meet you right where you are, whether you are in a front yard in Mississippi, on an airplane making a pilgrimage you don't know is a pilgrimage yet, in the midst of a hard day, or on the beach.

With this book Ife Afriye has once again created a sacred gathering, that all the systems of oppression we have survived told us was impossible. By sharing her own spiritual journey with the wisdom and experience of the high priestess she is, alongside the vulnerability of a person who has learned to practice compassion for every version of herself she has been along the way, she offers us a way into deeper relationship with ourselves, spirit, and the universe. Using the technology of the letter, she places you, kindred spirit reader, in circle with everyone else that matters, her own mind and soul, her ancestors, the elements, the ancient ones, her own daughters, mother earth. In this book you will find life-stories you can relate to, practical guidance for deepening your soul relationship to purpose and a model of inquiry and reflection that will allow you to find exactly the insights you need to find at this time. And if, like me, you plan to read this book again and again, it will show up to bless you where you are that day too

In fact, here I want to follow our great teacher and use the letter form myself:

Dear Sister Ife Afriye Kilimanjaro,

Your generosity in this book is boundless. You have once again created a space for us to be free. Gratitude to your ancestors, gratitude to your questions. Blessings upon your lineage, blessings upon every dream you are bringing into reality. Thank you for loving yourself with a love so expansive and multi-directional that it can include all of us. Thank you for being so honest and brave and humble and wise in this practice. Thank you for giving yourself the gift of yourself and sharing it. Thank you for giving me pathways to generations of love that are still coming home within my body, mind and soul. And thank you, in advance, on behalf of everyone who is reading this book now and everyone who ever will. Thank you for including us in this miracle.

Love and gratitude ALWAYS,

Your Sister Alexis Pauline Gumbs

Chapter One: Introduction

*Odomonkuma —
Why me?
Why this family, this body, these lands,
this moment in history?
Why now?*

There have been many moments in my life that have left me wondering how i got here. Not simply how i happened into certain experiences, encounters, or outcomes, but how it was that i came to exist in the first place. Why was i born? For what purpose did i enter into this world?

As i grew older, the breadth of these questions expanded beyond my individual personhood to include family and my people. For me these weren't merely abstract philosophical questions, rather they seemed to consistently re-emerge in moments of deep crisis within my life and in society. Often, they came when i was going through a tough moment, when i was feeling sad or anxious about something. But if i were to be honest with myself, this has been the central driving question of my life: What is *my* purpose?

In *Re-Membering Purpose* i delve into this question by seeking and assigning meaning to various experiences in my life that left me wondering what my purpose is now and what it has the potential to be in the future, assuming (which i do) that i had a choice in the matter. By doing this, i hope to offer inspiration, hope, and perhaps a little guidance to readers who may be asking themselves, their ancestors, or the Creator the same thing.

In addition to understanding what i came to this world to do, i am also curious about *how* i will do it (the methods or approaches of fulfilling my purpose), and what will it mean when all is said and done, as in when i leave this world. i am curious about the significance all of this has for the future of my soul, as well as the implications for my descendants and my ancestors. And finally, how do i know that i am on the right path and how will i know when i've fulfilled my purpose in life?

Before moving into these explorations of meaning and purpose, i want to note a compelling response Indian yogi and author Sadhguru Jaggi Vasudev offered to the question, "What is the purpose of life?" He said:

> "Isn't it fantastic that if there is no purpose, you have nothing to fulfill. You can just live. No but you want a purpose. And not a simple purpose. You want a god given purpose. It's very dangerous. People who think they have a God-given purpose are doing the cruelest things on the planet....because when you have a God-given purpose, life here becomes less important." (What is the Purpose of Life, 1/19/20)

In my understanding, Sadhguru offers that the impulse to define and live according to a purpose stems from the need to free oneself of the psychological, emotional, and material trappings which form when thought and emotion become more important than life (living life) itself. Purpose then becomes a way that the ego can feel good about itself, and the person goes on to organize life according to whatever they think their life purpose is. And in doing all of this, life is not being explored and lived fully.

i learned about Sadhguru and his work from one of his devotees while headed to a Vipassana meditation retreat in Chicago. It was a sunny September day in 2012 when i slid into the back seat of a taxi at O'Hare. The transition was notable, as the loud, bustling, chaotic airport energy gave way to a serene, calm, and quiet environment inside the car. As i settled into the back seat, i took a few deep breaths to slow myself down. It was at that point that i began to notice the sights and sounds within the car. Hanging from the mirror were what appeared to be Hindu symbols of spirituality. A small, framed photograph of a bearded man was perched on the dashboard. A gentle voice came through the speakers in a language i didn't recognize.

While i cannot recall all the details of what we discussed as he taxied me from the airport to my destination, i do remember that our conversation included him asking me how i was doing, me responding with how busy things were and how important this retreat was to me, and him responding with something quite simple and wise about happiness, agency, and personal choice. He invited me briefly into his life with stories about coming to Chicago and taxi driving. There was something quite striking about the simplicity of my driver's life, the joy he seemed to embody, and the depth of his wisdom. i craved these qualities in my own life, but they seemed quite unattainable: i was working multiple jobs as the sole provider for my family, felt deeply unsatisfied with how my life was going, and was too impatient and busy to cultivate wisdom. It was for these reasons that i wanted to learn more about him. To not be creepy, i settled for learning more about the ideas that shaped him. He referenced his guru a few times in the course of our conversation and suggested that i look up Sadhguru and the organization he founded.

What Sadhguru Jaggi Vasudev posits resonates with me as much as it unsettles me. What resonates with me is the limiting impact that purpose can have in a person's exploration of life and living fully, particularly if that purpose becomes the focus to the exclusion of all else. If, according to Sadhguru, my attention is narrowly focused on fulfilling a particular aim in life, then my ability, and even capacity, to be open to other possibilities and pursuits is potentially compromised. In pursuing a particular end, my mind is focused on that end, and my spirit-soul are unable to fully live under this kind of restrictive management. Indeed focusing in such a way limits the ability to see anything that is not on the path.

What is unsettling to me is how fundamentally outside of my orientation to the world this notion is. Everything is supposed to have purpose, right? i can't recall how or at what point in my life this existential expectation was seeded inside of me. All i know is that throughout my life, questions of purpose (and relatedly destiny) have not only surfaced time and time again in my consciousness, triggering lots of thought, internal conversations, journal entries and discussions with others, but also the pursuit of purpose and understanding my life's meaning seem to be some underlying theme in this incarnation of my life. Without a greater sense of purpose, why am i here? Why should i stay? In my personal and work lives, i've persistently grappled with these questions in my heart, with others, and in the creation of goals, objectives, and processes for evaluating progress. Does any of this have a place in my life? Does any of this *deserve* to have a place in my life?

For many years on my birthday, i would carve out time to assess alignment between what i felt was my higher calling and how i was living my life. I would review goals of the previous year and set new ones for the next. In my journal, i wrote all the mistakes i made, noted when i didn't meet a goal, recorded the lessons i learned, and composed suggestions for ways i could improve in the next year. Doing these annual assessments and goal setting activities felt important as they helped me to be accountable to myself and, i believed, would incrementally lead to the fulfillment of my life purpose.

To then be challenged by Sadhguru to consider life outside of such an organized way of existence felt a bit disorienting for me as it didn't fit within my way of being in this world. Does having purpose, or feeling as though i have a life purpose, preclude the emergence of other experiences and possibilities? In other words, is purpose truly a limiting force or can it be pursued in ways that allow for life to be lived fully?

These questions about purpose are ones that i've always asked. For decades, i've wondered what my purpose in being is and ought to be. Sometimes these questions came in deeply philosophical moments, where my mind curiously wandered down roads of soul searching and exploration. At other times, these questions emerged within painful circumstances of what felt like deep suffering. It was then that i desperately and feverishly sought understanding, and wondered, why stay? Each period of questioning gave rise to answers that seemed relevant and appropriate at the time and at the very least, provided just enough to keep me going. The questioning didn't stop. And the answers continued evolving.

What inspired me to pen this life quest, rather than continuing to work through these questions in my own mind, was my daughter Nia.

Throughout her life, my daughter Nia, whose name means purpose in Ki-Swahili, has served as a source of inspiration and learning by simply being who she is. It was about two months following her birth that her name came to me. After witnessing her observe the environment around her, reflect understanding in the deliberate movements of her tiny body, and express thoughtful willfulness, i knew she came to me and this world for a reason. And i knew that i needed to listen. And listen i did as she grew up, often imperfectly, but ultimately enough to support her growth and development into a deeply spiritual, insightful, and intelligent woman. In her youthful wisdom and with a gentle touch, Nia encouraged me to move these internal conversations from my head and into a place where i could observe and learn, and where others on similar journeys might also witness and learn.

At the time, i wanted to write about other things. My grounding in spirituality, training in sociology, interest in social relations of production,[1] and concerns about environmental justice and the climate crisis had me wanting to study and publish something within that nexus. But for some reason it felt as though a body of work much more intimate, more deeply personal, needed to come first, needed to be born first. Something within me called for a release of sorts, a letting go so that in the midst of the rawness and vulnerability i might find my source of creativity and inspiration, which could then energize all other subsequent work.

It felt inelegant in my body, like a plug that needed to be pulled, rather than an ethereal, light-filled beckoning. i remembered what novelist Ayi Kwei Armah advised.

In 2011, i spent a couple of months in Senegal to sit at the feet of Armah, whose life and work i regard highly. For years i found direction, companionship, and political groundedness in his writings because of their prioritization of African people's history, current realities, and renaissance should we overcome our greatest internal

---

[1] Social relations of production is a concept from the Marxian theoretical tradition that can be understood as the relationships between people as they meet the fundamental needs of their existence.

challenges as a people. I was so profoundly touched by Armah's work that i was driven to find my way to wherever in the world he was and humbly listen and learn. We did many things together and i learned so much, but one lesson in particular involved writing. He told me that to write well, to tell a story well, one had to be vulnerable. This doesn't mean that you have to tell all your business, but you have to open yourself up to the story that needs to be told.

So many ideas continued swirling around in my mind, and i remained indecisive about how to move forward, but i knew that my work would require vulnerability. I spent hours rereading journals that i've kept packed in boxes for over twenty years, looking for a hook. Should i write about specific events and encounters, such as my time with Armah or experiences and lessons running an African centered school on the eastside of Detroit? Should i organize my poetry by themes and arrange them in a book? These and other topics didn't quite take hold in me.

Not finding anything in the journals, i thought that perhaps i could build upon some of the work i contributed to various publications of University of Kmt Press, such as *Maat: Guiding Principles of Moral Living, African Time* or *Research Methods*. But i was saddled with more questions and uncertainty, given that my co-author and i had recently parted ways: How do we communicate about revisions to this shared body of work when our feelings of separation were so raw? Do i wait on identifying a writing project until after we could talk without stinging one another? How do we separate the material from ourselves? That i held these questions were clear indications that these weren't the next steps to take, at least not at this time.

So i asked my daughter, "What should i write about? What would you and your friends want to read?"

She responded, "I would want to read about you."

Ultimately, *Re-Membering Purpose* is a conversation spanning a lifetime between me and my soul, ancestors, spirit guides, and nature about the central guiding question of my life: What is my purpose?

What unfolds in a series of letters is a story and a journey that seem appropriate to share given the moment we live in. A moment in which many have and continue to suffer deeply because of racial injustices and violence, the COVID pandemic and loss of loved ones, joblessness, and more. A period in which many of the socio-economic and political solutions advanced by corporations and political leaders in the long run further damage the environment and public health. Many small businesses and individuals facing joblessness have been forced by circumstance to face their deepest fears, reexamine who they are, what they want out of life, and how to advocate for change. And within all of this, many are trying to understand where they fit.

With *Re-Membering Purpose,* i want to share approaches and tools i've used to define and discover meaning and purpose with the hopes that in doing so, others may at best feel supported in their own life by this body of work, or at the very least, be affirmed in the importance of their existence. And at a more fundamental level, i want to affirm orientations to the world (my own and others) that live beyond the linear, compartmentalized, and ahistorical ways society compels us to be.

For example, before trainings, schooling and initiations, something indescribable had led me to know, feel, and experience beings in the natural world as relatives. Listening to and holding conversations with pine trees and fungi, for example, were not strange to me. Nor did and do they now represent some sort of mental illness. What is normal and natural is connection with life in all its forms. And conversely, the separation from the natural world, separation from relationships with these relatives, is unnatural.

My spiritual grounding, as well as the language and concepts that help me to understand and articulate relationships and connection with the natural world, come from indigenous African spirituality. I have been given the titles of *Okomfo* (priest/spiritual healer) in the spiritual tradition of Akom (Ghana) and *Omo Awo* in the ancient tradition of Ifa (Nigeria) by my teachers and in recognition of my commitment to a lifetime of study and practice. These spiritual traditions have given me language to think about and articulate many of the relationships and experiences that i've had in life and that i know are possible. These traditions have also provided language and framing that is decidedly and historically Black African, which resonates deeply with who i am as a living spirit.

Throughout the text, i use the lowercase 'i' to reference myself, except at the beginning of sentences. For me, this practice of using a lower case i keeps me grounded in the understanding that as a human, i am no more or less important or bigger than other life forms. And the practice of using capital letters at the beginning of sentences represents that part of me that follows convention. In using these practices together, i aim to affirm that multiple and different realities can exist simultaneously alongside one another.

Recognizing the natural world as being full of kinship relations, rooting in African spirituality and ancestral reverence, and bucking grammatical conventions are only a few ways that i naturally live beyond societal conventions. Simultaneously, i have sought acceptance from purveyors of convention and tradition, often fumbling in my attempts to follow rules, because a part of me values being part of something more, something beyond rules. Within and beyond these different approaches, my search for purpose persists. And is my hope that those reading the letters on these pages who too live within and beyond convention will find something affirming and nourishing for their journeys. This book is for you. This book is for me. This book is for those yet to come.

Reflection Space

Please grab your journal and reflect on the questions, thoughts, words, word sequences and/or images that come to your mind as you reflect on the content of this chapter.

I offer the following prompts to get you started, if needed: What approaches and tools have you used to discover and assign meaning to various experiences you've had? In what ways do you conform to rules? How do you live and behave beyond or outside of those rules?

Chapter Two: A Letter to Reader, My Kindred Spirit

Dear Reader, my Kindred Spirit,

My daughter inspired me to write this, and the thought of you reading this kept me going. Perhaps it was knowing that there are people in this world, such as you, who are searching for answers to big questions and wanting to offer a reminder that all you seek is within you: the plural You, the most expansive You, the You that carries ancient knowledge in your DNA, the You that traveled with your ancestors before making your way into this lifetime and to whom You will return at some point, the You that is connected with life in all forms, the You that is in me. It is within all of these parts of yourself that answers to questions lay.

***TRIGGER WARNING:** In my own exploration of purpose, what i offer is an approach to answering the big questions in life and some nourishing food in the form of tools and tips for the journey. In the journey, there are issues that i raise and address that can be triggering and/or uncomfortable, depending on your life experiences and beliefs. For example, i speak to my own experiences of sexual abuse, abortion, and discrimination, as well as my own feelings of powerlessness and unworthiness. Reading this could potentially trigger those who have, or have had, similar experiences and feelings. I also center my Blackness, African spirituality, and assumptions about the world. Reading about this could make people who are oriented differently (i.e., people who don't center Blackness or who hold other spiritual beliefs) a bit uncomfortable. But i invite you to hang in there and take this journey with me because while our experiences and orientations may differ, there may be something to learn about yourself with the lessons and approaches i take in examining my own life. I know that i have most assuredly learned many things by listening to and observing the lives of others.

In moments where you notice discomfort arising in your mind-body-spirit, put the book down and breathe. If you need support, please reach out to get it. There are also resources listed at the end of the book that may help in this regard. If you are inspired to write, create, scream, laugh, connect, feel, or sit in silence, please do it. Tend to what is coming up. And continue the journey.

Above all, know that you got this. And i support you.

Love,
    Afriye

Chapter Three: Conversations With My Soul

i am
i am me because
you are
you are you because
i am

Dear Soul,

As far back as i can recall, i've wondered what my purpose in life is, even before i had that word in my lexicon. At 7 years old, i remember asking Grandfather Pine, after climbing as high as i could and nestling in his wooded arms, *"Why me?"*

"Why me?" i cried inside when under the threat of a beating i was forced by a caregiver to eat spaghetti with chunky tomatoes (which i despised as an 8 year old), along with my own vomit because i couldn't stomach it.

"For what reason am i still here?" looped inside of my mind as i popped pill after pill with the intention to die, not realizing that aspirin wouldn't do the job. I was 14.

"I know why i am here," i thought when at 21 i held my newborn for the very first time, looked into her big brown eyes, and experienced that indescribable rush of love for this being that only moments before lived inside of me. But i soon realized that she was only part of it, part of the meaning and purpose of my life. I knew this because the questions would continue to surface in moments,

voices, and ways that the answer of my daughter's life didn't quite fulfill. Plus, she had her own purpose to fulfill that may include me but isn't about me.

I seek answers from you, Soul, about this bigger question of purpose, beyond parenthood. And while you're at it, can you also tell me why i chose to return to this world, in this particular moment in history, to the particular parents i have? And when i was making these decisions, did i agree to complete particular tasks, have certain experiences, or learn specific lessons? If any part of the answer to that question is yes, how will i know that i've accomplished these things, therefore fulfilling my purpose?

It feels kind of weird talking with you in this way, because we are, after all, in the same body. But at the same time, we are different.

You see, i've thought long and hard about this and feel pretty certain that i am the thinker and you are the feeler. I provide intellect and reason, you provide emotion. I give us—you , me and this body we share—a sense of individuality and personhood, whereas you are more connected with the spiritual, ancestral, and emotional parts of us. Sometimes i don't quite know all that you do, but you seem to fill our body with life, energy, and direction. And since i am providing distinctions here, i might as well tell you what i know about this body we share. It is our public face to the world, a living organism that responds to and influences us through sensory inputs and responses to external and internal stimuli. Have i understood this

correctly?
    And can you tell me what i came here to do?

Love,
    Mind

Mind,

You are young, curious. This is good. Continue asking questions and follow the paths in the directions created by your pursuit of answers. Be open to what you see, humble with what you learn, and discerning in what you think you know.
    You are also presumptuous and naive. This is because you are young, yet you don't know it. If you want answers, still yourself so that you can listen; quiet yourself so that you may hear; humble yourself so that you may learn.

Soul

> *if i chose to be born
> what was the purpose i hoped
> to fulfill? why now?*

Dear Soul,

That stings a little because i am the one who has had to face the world each day of our life, a world that values intellect and reason, where it matters what i think and not how i feel. But i hear you, too. Perhaps that is why i keep coming back to you with these questions, because something about this emphasis on me to the diminishment of you feels imbalanced. Clearly you are my elder, and as such, you are wiser. i respect that.

   I do hope that you, Soul, will bear with me in this search for purpose and meaning, as asking questions sometimes makes me seem a little stupid and leaves me vulnerable, not knowing something that perhaps i should know…you know? But i also know that asking questions builds a kind of honesty within myself, because nothing is off the table and i am free to be curious. I think that the search for answers is where growth and development happens, right?

   The search for answers about purpose and meaning, in particular, has led me to learn about and adopt certain practices that quiet my often-incessant internal conversations. I have taken initiative to deepen meditation and Kemetic yoga practices so that i may better hear you, Soul, in the midst of all the distractions and demands of the world. I was also looking to these practices to help me quiet myself long enough to listen to and understand messages from other parts of this body we share, such as the heart, muscles and gut. Meditation and yoga give me tools to listen, take notice and find solutions. For example, when the stomach informs me that it aches, i can explore if the source is stress, anxiety, poor combination of foods, or something else, and then apply an appropriate remedy, like pausing for deep breaths, calibrating my work load, refraining from eating so close to bed time, or implementing some other practice.

I've wanted a better understanding of this relationship between us, as it will help me to gain insights into why i am here in this lifetime and how purpose connects with destiny beyond this life. Why is this important to me? Because without this knowledge, i don't know that i would want to be here. I need you to help me remember why we are here and re-member our dismembered memories, to which i believe you have access. Knowing why we are here and what we came to do might lead me to take greater care when making decisions that impact the body that holds us together. Perhaps then i may listen more deeply or better attend to the needs of the body we share as they arise. Perhaps i may take better care of us, listen to and honor the myriad ways our body speaks, letting me know when certain foods create harm, when certain relationships pose health risks, when stress is more than a response and instead has become a way of living: all of these things impact the longevity of our time on this planet, and therefore our capacity to live long enough to realize the purposes that are defined, redefined, met again, and so on.

Can you help me? Will you join me on this journey?

I know that i was presumptuous with what i wrote before, implying that i chose to be born. How could that be when i only came into existence after our brain formed? Perhaps i took something that you showed me and claimed it as my own. I am ready to still myself. I am ready to listen. I am ready to learn.

Sincerely,
    Mind

Mind,
    This is a start. I am listening.

Soul

*Each day i call forth
the very best of myself
May i be ever true
to the path of my calling*

Dear Soul,

Several blood lines run through this body that you and i share. Through our mother passed the blood of generations of mainly Black people. And from at least the last five generations that i have been able to trace, roots were planted, uprooted, and replanted in such places as Capitol Heights, MD; Washington D.C.; Detroit, MI; Ann Arbor, MI; Chicago, IL; Lexington, KY; Baton Rouge, LA; and Higginsville, MO. Before that, my mom's people came largely from Nigeria, Scotland, and Cameroon.

As it turns out, the person i grew up believing was our father did not contribute to the genetic stew that led to our formation. That was an interesting discovery, though not entirely unexpected.

In my late 20's, i began to suspect that the person i grew up thinking was our father was not. I simply didn't see us in him or his family. There were no likenesses or mannerisms that we shared with anyone. Not that it isn't unheard of, or even uncommon i imagine, that children don't share obvious likenesses or mannerisms with a parent. Similarity itself is certainly not enough to base paternity. But it was enough for me to ask our mother. *Is it possible that he is not my father?* to which she responded after a thoughtful pause, *yes*.

For some time i searched for my biological father, even finding one newspaper reference about him, but was unable to make contact. So, i left it alone. Perhaps it wasn't true, perhaps it wasn't time, perhaps i wasn't ready. When ancestry.com confirmed this fact nearly ten years later through a sibling match, i was satisfied that my suspicion was confirmed, but i noticed shifts in our body with this discovery.

The words i have for these feelings are: overwhelm, curiosity, apprehension, interest, frustration and anger. My interpretation of these feelings was that we were overwhelmed because i created a fantasy that my biological father was Black, but instead was white, a realization that led to important questions about this side of my family. Essential questions like: Were they racists? Were they homophobes?

I was not going to subject myself to another round of rejection, but i wanted to know who they were. Who is this sister that we have and what is she like? And i understood the feelings of frustration and anger as having to do with this discovery happening so late in life. I, like so many, grew up without knowing my father.

There have been moments when i've wondered what it would have been like to have a father in my life. Neither the one who i thought was my father, nor the biological one, were present, and worse, both were absent in ways that would never have allowed a relationship with us to seed. As i learned about the bio dad, i discovered that he shared the same kind of mental illness as the presumed dad, which left them moving in and out of worlds, unable to show up for the people in their lives, distant and unable to connect. Whatever longing for a father that we might have had is senseless, practically useless, knowing what schizophrenia does to a person.

We never met before he passed away a few months ago, but in what i've been able to learn about him and his family and the pictures i've seen is that we look like and are like them in so many ways. It has felt delicious at times and overwhelming at others to see myself in that family. They are educators, artists, and activists. They are deeply spiritual (not religious) with ancestral homes in Scotland, England, and Russia (Ashkenazi Jews) before arriving in New York three generations ago. All of that lives in us.

I've laid out for you the very brief bloodline trail that converged to make us; not that you needed me to do that, but i needed to lay out our coming into being in a logical and chronological order because that is how i understand things. I needed to be able to map out the people who made possible our existence, and within that, explore with you how we came to be with a mind, soul and body that uniquely makes us who we are.

At some point a young, beautiful woman and burly young man were drawn to one another in mutual attraction, passion, and youthful love. She was only months out of high school, taking classes at Wayne State University and trying to find her place in the world. He was a member of a religious cult that had come to Detroit to save souls. I learned from mom after confirming that he was my bio dad, that they met on the corner of Mack and Woodward Avenue in a parking lot where he worked as an attendant. Immediately they were drawn to one another, spiritually, emotionally, and sexually. As fate would have it (along with hot sex[2]), determined sperm found its way into a receptive egg and rapid multiplication of embryonic cells began. And the body that we—Mind and Soul—would come to inhabit began to form.

What i want to know from you, Soul, is how we came to be this person called Ife Afriye and why was it that we were born? At what point did you enter this growing body? And assuming you entered before me, at what point did i come?

From what you've shown me in meditation and study, you began a lengthy process of entering the body when it clearly had human features but was still early in its formation. Is it correct to assume that conjoining at this time, this early in the pregnancy, provided sufficient time and space for you to transition from your ethereal residence alongside the ancestors to a new home (body) with much greater density? I imagine that in addition to the time it took to travel across worlds, you needed time to get to know the body that you were inhabiting, even as you filled it with your life and became one with it. So much remains unknown about this process. But is this what happened? Is this the order it happened in?

---

[2] Hopefully the sex was good, as I would like to think that my conception came from an amazingly passionate encounter.

As you know, meditation was where we had our clearest conversations, when we could have them. Well, perhaps it was more like i was talking and you were showing me embodied images, colors, feelings, sounds and movements—matter and energy in motion—to help me make sense of it all. Admittedly, it was hard for me to quiet myself enough to listen and to hear you. It takes time for me to settle down because of all the thoughts, questions, and sometimes worries that circulate. I appreciate your patience with me. And i received what you gave me.

And in my intellectual exploration, Soul, it felt as though you guided me to scholarly works that showed me that African people have been exploring existential questions since antiquity. For example, i found such life in the works of Cheik Anta Diop, Theophile Obenga, Ayi Kwei Armah and Per Ankh Press, who introduced to generations of people a Black African civilization that fashioned philosophies, sciences, and other cultural systems and practices. They approached our history with such scientific rigor and ancestral care. I appreciate that we focused primarily on the work of African scholars who were grounded in the cosmologies and wisdoms of their aboriginal ancestors and eschewed attempts to fit into European intellectual frameworks.

By directing me to these and other works by African people and their diasporic kin, it seemed as if you knew how important it was for me to ground in the best of what our people offered history on these questions, as opposed to beginning this search for purpose and meaning in the intellectual products of Europeans.

One thing that i learned was that while so much of this process of *soul landing* (which to me means when the soul enters the body) is unknown and believed to be one of the divine mysteries hidden from human consciousness, the soul resides in the company of other souls before being directed by the Creator to return to earth to continue carrying out its destiny. To the Akan,[3] the pregnancy is the process of a soul transitioning into the earth plane from the spiritual plane. The soul receives its charge from the aspect of God that bestows destiny and then moves into the growing body of the embryo, animating it with life. It is believed that the soul is an ancestor that moves through bloodlines.

While i cannot know the precise moment at which you began to ease your way into the growing embryo in our mother's womb, at a certain point, you transitioned in and later, i entered. You moved into this new suit, this living organism that is our body, and i think, carried with you both the memory of the past (the ancestral part of us) and the imprint of our destiny.

For purposes of this exploration of purpose, i understand that we all came together in our mother's womb: The process of biological life set into motion through the passion of my parents. You began your journey from the spirit world into the body sometime at the

---

[3] Ephirim-Donkor, A., *African Spirituality: On Becoming Ancestors*. University Press of America. 2011.

beginning of the first trimester of development. This is based off the assumption that i didn't develop until after you joined the body and the brain was fully formed, which was sometime at the end of the second or beginning of the third trimester.

Arriving at this understanding makes me wonder about what might have happened if my mother decided to not carry us to term. She was only eighteen when learning about the new life growing inside and had just begun taking college classes at Wayne State University. Even though her choices were limited as Roe v. Wade hadn't yet been decided,[4] women at that time who were determined to end a pregnancy had their ways (though there was always a risk of sickness, infection or even death). I wonder if had my mom been able to terminate this pregnancy, would my soul have chosen to come at another time? And i wonder if the embryo that i aborted years ago ever received its soul?

It was 1989. As a teenager, freshly out of high school and pregnant, i thought that we didn't have any choices, our only option being a life of welfare, multiple children, absent fathers, and loneliness. This was what i saw around us at the time. If other possibilities existed for us, i didn't know, and this led to sadness in our body. Just days after graduation, we began college as part of the

---

[4] **Roe vs. Wade** was a landmark decision in January 1973 in which the Supreme Court ruled that the U.S. Constitution conferred the right to have an abortion. Unfortunately this decision was overturned on **June 24, 2022.**

Upward Bound Bridge program. I was inspired by the possibilities that lay ahead: taking interesting classes like creative writing, biology, and philosophy; learning about and meeting people from places i had only read about in books, like Africa, India and China; and one day traveling the world. But youthful carelessness threw an ax in that glass wall, the shattering of my dreams reminding me that such possibilities are for people who can afford them and not some poor Black kid in Toledo.

Somehow a combination of forces shaping who we were at seventeen led us into a relationship with a handsome young man who graduated the year before. Though my memory falls short of how we became interested in one another, what we talked about, and how we spent time together, i know that i really liked him. He was tall, dark brown, well-groomed, and although he was kind, he had a rough edge—he had seen some battles, been in a few fights—and he had a car.

Sometimes he would pick us up from school and we would head to his house, where we would bypass the front door and make a beeline to the side door, which led directly to his basement bedroom. There we would spend time having what i thought at the time was really good sex: it was my choice, there was no pain, and it kind of felt good. In my teenage mind, that was all it took. Despite our efforts to prevent the seeding of the next generation, that was what indeed happened. A condom must have broken or maybe we failed to use one at some point. i can't remember. At graduation, i didn't yet know that new life was growing inside of us. All i knew was that in just a few days we would begin college.

Excited and hopeful, we (you and i, Soul) moved into our dorm room at the university in town on the Sunday following my Friday graduation. Even though the university i attended was only a few miles away from home—where our mom, her husband and our siblings lived—we were excited to be there, in our new, albeit temporary, abode. Remember how ecstatic we were to be in a place where we could be as grown as i thought we were, a place where serious grown-ups congregated, a place where there wasn't a bunch of foolishness and drama (or so i thought at the time), a place where we could learn and grow from and with others?

My dormmate Sharonda and i knew one another from high school and learned that we would share space a few weeks earlier when the orientation information about the Upward Bound's Bridge Program landed in our mailboxes. Though we didn't know one another well, we knew who one another was because we had a class or two together. What i noticed about Sharonda in high school was that she was studious, somewhat quiet and quite shapely, often having to sit uncomfortably on the edge of the chair since classroom desks were made for smaller bodies. At times i wondered what it was like to live in such a large body in such a judgmental place as high school. I saw the looks people gave her and i often thought of Mom in those moments.

Mom, too, had a rather robust body, and i was well

familiar with the judgments, rudeness, and cruelty that she sometimes faced from onlookers, passersby, grocery store clerks, and more. I couldn't imagine what it must have felt like as a teenager. I asked Sharonda one day how she dealt with the stares. "I just ignore them," she said, looking out the window. I remember that moment so clearly because there was an uncomfortable feeling that filled the room, something that felt like a mix of pain, resignation, and fury. I didn't probe as it seemed the conversation ended.

A couple of weeks into college life, acute sensitivity to smells and certain foods developed, leaving me persistently nauseous. Each day i threw up with such force that our face speckled with small red dots. I knew this could mean only one thing.

Anxiety, fear, and hopelessness filled my body. I didn't know what to do, except to accept the fate meted out to poor Black girls like me. This initial reaction of acceptance ran through my mind the stories of others that i thought would be my story too: this would be the first of several children i would have from different fathers and that the fate of welfare, financial hardship, and loneliness lay ahead.

I remember returning to my dorm after the diagnosis full of disappointment and rage. Not only was i pregnant, but had gonorrhea too! Both weighed heavy on me. How do i process these feelings of betrayal around the STD? Clearly my boyfriend had to have been with someone else without protection, putting all of us at risk. What was he thinking? What was i thinking? How would i tell my mom that i would have to drop out of college because i was pregnant, especially after all of the work we did to get to this point? How do i face my younger siblings who were looking up to me, taking guidance from my actions? What would people think of me, my mom's friends, the neighborhood gossip, the people at the church i no longer attended? One of my greatest fears—and greatest causes of stomach pains—was that i would now fulfill the low expectations that i was certain people already had of me.

I called my boyfriend, angry about the STD and embarrassed about the pregnancy, as though that part of the situation was my fault. Before even talking to him, i decided that i would do this parenting thing without him because clearly he wasn't ready and clearly that is what women do; it is what the women in my family have always done. We take care of the children that men, for whatever reason, are unable to show up for. In spite of the emotions raging inside our body about all of this, i spoke dryly, letting him know about the STD, that he had gotten it from somewhere else and that he should get treated. I told him about the pregnancy, that i didn't know what i was going to do and that i couldn't be with him anymore.

I hung up and cried.

Sharonda was sitting on her bed across from me the entire time, sending us reassuring looks of support. "What are you going to do now?" she asked when the tears cleared. "I don't know," i said, "but i have to tell my mom."

That Saturday, i caught the bus home to inform my family. All i can remember about telling Mom was her silence, for days. Her clear disappointment in me hung like an albatross around my neck, making it hard to breathe. In her silence, Mom left information for the Women, Infants, and Children (WIC) Program near the door of her house. It was her way of suggesting that i sign up soon, so that i could get support from the government. I felt awful. I never wanted to get on welfare as an adult and yet here we were.

Granny was venomous toward me. I think that was how she showed her disappointment, by being really mean. "How could you be so careless? How could you mess up this chance at a different life? Well, I guess you're gonna be like your mama!" The way she spoke to me stung. Regarded as a college student in one moment, i quickly became a hoe. I became someone that wasn't going to amount to anything in life, someone for whom pregnancy was bound to happen at some point. My grandmother's disappointment in my mother's choices and circumstances poured into me. The venomous behind-the-back talking weighed heavy on my spirit. Hearing such destructive attacks on my character made it impossible to be around my granny and granddaddy. I caught the bus back to the dorm Sunday afternoon, staring despondently out of the window the entire time, my rumination so deep, I nearly missed my connecting bus downtown. Glad to be in the dorm for another month and a half, i stayed away as much as possible to avoid the line of fire.

"Have you considered abortion?" My aunt asked me. Aunt T was the refreshing light in the midst of this dark time in my life. She called me when the family gossip train made its way to her. Aunt T and i were pretty close and had been since she and her son returned to Detroit from Redwood City when i was in middle school. My siblings and i would visit her during the summer in Detroit and hang out in the neighborhood. Frank and direct, she always talked to me like an adult. We didn't always agree, but the conversations were always honest and i loved her for that.

Aunt T had called to ask what was going on, who was this boy and how i was doing before springing that question on me. It wasn't until that moment, nearly three months into our pregnancy, that i even understood that abortion was a choice i could make. Though i knew that abortions existed, the stories i'd heard were scary and always ended with a woman or girl dying on a table from botched coat hanger attempts to terminate the pregnancy or subsequent infections. These stories had pushed the idea of abortion so far out of my mind that when faced with the reality of my situation, which required the consideration of all the possibilities, it didn't even enter into my consciousness.

Aunt T opened my world up with that simple question. I went to an abortion clinic in Toledo. At the time it didn't require my mother's knowledge even though i was only seventeen. They "counseled" me and told me that i was almost past the date by which they could give the abortion. To ensure that i was certain about this decision, they made me look at brightly colored, detailed pictures of what the baby looked like at nearly three months and then what it would look like if unnaturally chopped up and removed from my womb. They said that i could return the next day (or in three days, i don't remember which) after thinking more about it and that i should only return if i was certain i wanted to go through it. It was terrifying seeing those colorful posters of dead baby body parts, all bloody and broken. I didn't consider myself a murderer, but they made me feel that way sitting there, alone, taking all of this in. Their "counseling" worked. I decided to not return.

My aunt called me a few days later to check on me. "What did you decide?" she asked. I thought back to my experience. "It just doesn't feel possible," i said. Unwilling to see her niece follow roads that she and others have been down, my aunt said, "I know where you can do it here in Detroit. I know a place, and I will help you."

Scared and grateful, i accepted her support, along with her intention to give me a chance to move through life with a renewed sense of hope.

I can't say if this was the right decision. Simply that it was a decision. I can't say what life would've been like if this child was able to be born and grow. Nor can i pine over that which will forever be unknown. But in its short life, this baby connected me with the generations of women and girls who've had to make difficult decisions about their bodies and the resulting implications for their personal futures, as well as their families and communities.

As i look back at this moment in my life while writing this letter to you, Soul, i wonder what came of the soul that might have animated the embryo i terminated.

About seven years ago i had a dream in which i saw my maternal grandmother, who passed in 2005, standing in the doorway of a house. The sun's brilliance shone a spotlight on her as she walked onto the porch smiling. Granny lovingly cradled a baby in her arms. As she looked in my direction, she slightly lifted the bundle to show me that she was caring for the life that i gave up. There was something in her eyes that gave me permission to release lingering doubts about the decision i made all those years ago. There was something in her disposition that told me she would be there for me in the spirit world in ways she wasn't able to be there for me in the living world.

As i reinterpret that dream through my evolving understanding of the relationship between the mind, soul and body, i wonder if perhaps the soul of this child began its journey into the womb at the time of the extraction. Memories of the abortion and the months following are flooding my mind: i remember the intensely painful cramping and blood loss that grew stronger and heavier in the weeks and months following the abortion. I remember visiting a doctor to find out what was wrong with me after the pain made it nearly impossible to walk and i could no longer staunch the flow of blood and clots coming out of me. I remember passing out in the doctor's office. Groggily, i woke toto hands lifting my body from the floor to a hospital gurney. I remember being hospitalized and infused with antibiotics to address the growing infection in our body from the abortion and with blood to replenish what had been lost. I was there for nearly a week.

I don't recall if anyone came, other than my ex-boyfriend, who hovered over me, asking if i was seeing someone else and checking the pulse in my neck to see if i was telling the truth. It was horrible.

Was i being punished for making this decision? Was all this pain and blood loss a consequence of a disrupted energy transmission? Or was it simply that the equipment in the abortion clinic was not sufficiently sterilized? Whether the post-abortion trauma i experienced was due to these or other causes i will never know. But something about the presence of my Granny in my dream let me know that i need not worry. She is holding that part of me safely in her arms. And while i cannot know what or whose soul would've come through me all those years ago, or what its destiny would've been, my hope and prayer is that it has had an opportunity (or will have one in the future) to continue its journey towards fulfillment of its destiny.

Feeling a bit clearer about origins, or perhaps more accurately, feeling satisfied with what i know and don't know about how we came into being, i want to return to the question of my purpose. If there are conditions for having a purpose in life to be met, i imagine that having life or being alive would be first. Clearly, as i sit here directing our hands to write this letter, we are alive with a mind and soul in this body. And for a time, we (Mind,

Soul, and Body) grew together in the dark place of the womb until it came time to enter this world. A variety of circumstances favored our birth, setting into motion a multitude of other experiences that would shape and be shaped by our/my existence, decisions, and actions. Indeed, this Soul Train[5] began the journey of fulfilling a purpose that i hope you, Soul, will help me discover.

Searching,
    Mind

> Mind,
>
> You are trying to understand matters that are beyond your capacity. But this does not mean you are any less valuable to our community[6] than anyone else. It is you who make it possible for us to live together in this world, interact with other people and environments, learn through various intellectual media and material, navigate material realities, and feed critical information to the rest of us in this body community.
>
>   You reason and draw logical conclusions from observations and study. You do this a lot. Sometimes too much, but you are learning to sit back and allow other intelligences within our body

---

[5] My birth happened to fall in the same month and year that the first episode of Soul Train aired.

[6] By community, i mean 'mind-body-soul community.'

community to share. Does this study, reflection, meditation, and consultation with me mean that you now understand when and how I enter? I can neither confirm nor deny your conclusions. There are memories that even I cannot access. Besides they have no relevance to us. What is of greater significance is how we live and that we learn, grow, listen, and do.

That is all for now.
Soul

I Forgive

*I forgive myself for
all the judgment,
negative thoughts and the self loathing*

*I forgive myself for
trying to harm with
food and alcohol*

*I forgive myself for
being careless with my life*

*I forgive myself for
the decisions i've made that have
caused harm and sadness*

*I forgive myself for
all the excuses i've made in my life*

*I forgive myself for
not valuing my life
- 7/7/18*

Dear Soul,

I want to do my part to fulfill our purpose in life. For me this translates into learning as much as i can about all things related to our time together so that i can contribute where appropriate. Your response to my last letter makes me think about the struggles we've had within our body community—our internal struggles—and the implications for understanding our purpose AND fulfilling it.

Funny thing, Soul. You chose to enter a growing fetus that would spend many years engaging in internal struggles on multiple levels, and often simultaneously. If you at one point sat among the ancestors, then you must have been able to see some of this beforehand and therefore could have made another choice, right? You must have been able to anticipate what it would mean to live between extremes in a world that values one side over another: white over Black, male over female, straight over fluid, wealthy or middle class over economically poor.

We were born under an astrological sign whose essence is to see both sides of things (Libra), to a biracial couple who faced at the family level, the racism and rejection reflected in society writ large. We united within the body that would be gendered female, but whose essence bucked against the social conventions of our generation. We were born into an economic class that informed us daily that whatever rights we thought we had to healthy food, running water, access to working utilities, safety in community and dignity was misplaced; only those worthy of such privilege because they had greater wealth and material resources deserved these things. We were born as a girl who felt more fluid in her attraction and sexuality, but couldn't accept this because it stood in opposition to what was acceptable.

Somehow the reality of who we were never seemed to align with how we were supposed to be according to the norms and standards of society, how we were expected to be to get along in this world and find acceptance. This created tension between you and i, Soul.

I wanted to fit in, whereas you simply wanted to be.

Over the years, these internal tensions would arise in moments that made me wonder not only why we were born, but also why we chose to stay. You know that i wanted to end it all many times because, as i look back on it, we never seemed to agree with one another about who and how to be in this world. You wanted self-acceptance, but i needed to be accepted by others. You wanted to play football with the boys, but when the nun said girls didn't do that, i didn't want us to get in trouble; i made us comply. You wanted to dance, paint, and create other forms of art, you wanted to attend art school, but i didn't think it was practical. We needed a job, multiple jobs to pay for a place to live and a car. You wanted to travel and live in other countries, but i didn't see how that was possible and practical given that we were poor. You wanted to hang out in the countryside, communing with trees, growing food and flowers, but how would we live, Soul? You trusted spirit and i trusted people, even when they let me down.

Your desire, Soul, for us to be true to who we were didn't fit within the family, community, and society to which i was trying to adapt. In essence, it seemed as if you wanted us to be truly free. That is noble and beautiful, but the world we live in doesn't support that.

I wanted us to walk along the acceptable paths: go to college, get a good job, live in a nice neighborhood, get married to a decent man, have children, and find happiness with that. I set us up with men, you struggled inside the whole time, sending me messages that you'd rather be with a woman. I set us up with good, stable jobs, but you sent messages to me that something was missing but wouldn't say what it was. I made it possible for us to travel to many different places, but you let me know that the visits weren't long enough. You let me know that you needed time to learn the culture and language of our human and plant kin, you needed more time for connection, and you needed greater distance from concrete-filled cities. But the jobs are in those cities. Stability and what i thought was security was fueled by work in those cities. How can we live if we are not working? How can we take care of our family?

In so many instances like these, tensions would grow—at times slowly, other times more quickly—until they culminated into a major change or sometimes a crisis, such as a breakup, job change, or relocation. And it was there that i would ask questions of you, of the ancestors, and of God themselves, in some sort of attempt to understand what was going on, why we couldn't agree on how to be in the world, why you continued to stubbornly refuse to follow my orders, and why couldn't we be just like everybody else?

Even as we navigated our internal tensions, life still happened: bills, jobs, relationships, school, etc. And in this life, various experiences left me asking why life seemed to be so hard, so depressing, so suffocating. Why did i never seem to earn enough to pay all the bills each month? Was it in our purpose to struggle? Was it our purpose to feel unwanted, unaccepted, worthless, and unworthy during our tenure on this earth?

More often than i want to admit, i longed for a relationship with my father's family (or the person i thought was my father). But it felt as though they never wanted to know me, like they never wanted me. This longing for acceptance and searching for belonging had its roots in this rejection i felt by the white family who seemed unsettled by my mother's Blackness. I never seemed to belong, nor be accepted, regardless of how hard i tried as a child. I often questioned how we were supposed to navigate the traumas we experienced as a child, the intimate violations that certainly left a lingering impact on our spirit.

For example, why was i left to sort through the confusion, fear, and excitement, when under the care of a family friend, one of their teenage sons pinned me down and forced himself on me, touching me in embarrassing ways, while threatening me to not say anything? i was six years old. I didn't know what was happening. I didn't know that the impact of these encounters over a three-year period would leave me feeling confused and violated, lacking healthy boundaries, and silencing myself. I didn't know that i would be scarred and that those scars would be ripped open again and again by another family friend and another.

I know, Soul, that not everything was bad. We share memories that are positive, affirming, and life giving. The birth of my siblings was always joyful: playing with them, watching them grow over the years and sharing important moments, like when the oldest of my younger brothers preached a sermon at four years old on the steps of the church stage, or when the second brother one graduated from college many years later, or when the youngest lost his first tooth. There was beauty and affirmation in the simplest of memories that emerge from countless positive experiences as an older sister. Even the tough moments reminded me that we, in our body community, were part of something larger and more significant: a family.

But something would inevitably remind me that these moments of joy were miniscule given the broader context of our lives. A moment would reinforce negative messages that also made a home in my understanding of family.

The inability to pay a bill would lead to water shutoffs. The message: if we didn't have money, we didn't deserve basic necessities.

My unsuccessful attempt to convince my white father's sister that it didn't matter if he couldn't take us shopping, we still wanted to visit. The message: your brown body is not welcome here.

The family friend who climbed on top of me over and over again even though i said no. The message: you have no say over your body.

As i sit here writing, i am carried to a memory. I am in my early 20s, riding a Greyhound. I am returning to

Toledo from Washington, D.C. after visiting Howard University, which would be my future alma mater. This was only months after giving birth to my daughter. Breasts overflowing with milk, i was grown. A mother., i'm seated next to a large white man. Older. Quiet. Nothing seemed unusual. It was late and everyone was preparing for an overnight journey. Tired, i looked forward to getting some sleep before the first of a few transfers. I fell asleep.

I wake up to a hand grabbing my upper thigh, where it joins my hip, and making its way into my crotch. I grab it hand and move it away. Told him to stop it. But i remain. Frozen. Unable to move. A short time passes and i feel it again. And again, i grab his hand and move it. Telling him to stop. But remaining frozen. Not yelling. Afraid to draw attention to something i couldn't believe was happening. At the next stop i change seats..

A young lady sits next to him, in the seat i vacated. I thought i must do something. If i wasn't brave enough to report him to the Greyhound driver, i could at least warn her about him. I couldn't get the words out. They were stuck in my throat. Finally, when i could take it no more, i blurted out inarticulately and uncharacteristically loud that she should be careful of him because he has roaming hands. She didn't hear me at first, or perhaps she had a hard time piecing together the raggedy way i was speaking. I said it again. And she heard me. And thanked me. The man simply sat there with his eyes closed, as though he didn't hear a thing.

Shit. Why didn't i have the courage to say

something or do something besides just sit there? Why didn't i have the courage to elbow his throat or break his fingers or simply report him? I look back on that experience (and others) and think about a million things i could've done to advocate for myself, to fight, but instead i silenced myself. My tongue numb as the memories of all the warnings and admonitions to not tell when older and elder family friends touched me in inappropriate ways, climbed on top of me, watched me in perverted silence. Silenced to speak about what these people were doing. Silenced. Feeling worthless and without voice.

I tried in many ways to convince myself otherwise: trying to do things right, not make mistakes, make good decisions, be morally upright, have control over things and be in control. And like a trained circus animal, whenever i did something, said something, or experienced something that was different than how i thought it should go when anything turned out less than perfect in my estimation, then i returned to the emotional, and at times physical, self-flagellating practices of beating myself up, cutting myself, and drinking until i found a sense of relief or was simply too out of it to care. Even successes were short lived in my mind because somehow the internal judgment would quickly remind me that i didn't earn it and that i was nothing more than that worthless, poor Black girl-child that wouldn't amount to anything.

I don't recall that these words were ever spoken by my mom or other family members. Rather the experiences of sexual abuse, rejection by my father's family, and being told by teachers and society that girls are supposed to behave certain ways (that were contrary to my nature) conspired together to keep me in line.

It was all part of a perfect storm, the trauma i've experienced, the unhealthy ways i tried to cope, and the ultimate silencing of myself and my needs. What did it all mean? What was i supposed to find in the calm of that storm?

In retrospect, i look upon each moment, each experience, as a valuable opportunity to learn. If each experience serves as a teacher, what did i learn? What am i learning as i reexamine these moments in my life?

In writing this letter to you, i am remembering recurring themes in my life that seem to emerge as triggered emotional responses.. There are the negative emotions that i have struggled with for years, including self-loathing, self-criticism, and judgment, fear, and negative self-talk. I can understand people, experiences, etc. teaching me valuable lessons along the way, but the issues i just mentioned are like forces within that have sought to undermine all the good that i've tried to do in life, all the ways i've tried to evolve and grow, all the moments where i have actually felt like i did something valuable or meaningful.

As i look back on the painful experiences, i've often wondered, what was it that has anchored us to this existence, particularly when i've wanted to part ways and return to the source? In the most challenging of moments in our life, what was it that has kept us tethered to this plane of existence? Was it that you, Soul, knew we were so much more than the sum of our experiences? Was it that you knew we would get through this and so much more? Was it you who knew we would become whole again?

I would love some guidance here as i am feeling raw and vulnerable. Feelings aren't things that i generally experience as they don't precisely fall in my domain, but somehow they are, with you, right now.

Vulnerable and searching,
    Mind

Mind,

Some things we choose. And some things we don't. With both we have the power to decide what to do with the experiences we have and information we glean.

Teachers come in many forms. Recall the message from the labyrinth: forgive yourself, forgive others, trust, do.

May your truth be revealed,
Soul

Nana Asuo Gyebi

Oh Great One
Great Warrior and Diplomat
Carrier of the double-edged sword
Help me to know which part of me to bring forward
when duty calls

Oh Great One
Protector and healer
keeper of earth and spirit medicines
help me to know the tools to bring forward

I humble myself to your guidance[7]

Dear Soul,

Respectfully, as the elder among us, can you give me a little more? Can you answer my questions directly, instead of giving me more to think about? Sometimes i just want you to tell me the answer so that i can take a break from doing the work of figuring things out. Don't get me wrong, i appreciate the messages and all. I just...well, i just thought i'd be further along at this age and stage in my life, with more answers than questions. But here we are.

And really, i do appreciate your responses. Although they are short, this exchange with you has afforded me the freedom to ask all the questions i've been

---

[7] Nana Asuo Gyebi is a deity in the African Spiritual Tradition of Akom that is known for many things, including protection, plant medicines and diplomacy.

grappling with and process the myriad experiences, particularly the more difficult ones, that have shaped me. And i feel closer to knowing my purpose…i think.

Looking back on my life, it seems as though elements of purpose revealed themselves at various moments, including and perhaps especially during the most difficult times. All along you, Soul, as well as our ancestors and spirit guides were giving me keys, granting access to new information through various experiences, lessons and teachers; even teachers that took the form of trauma, challenging moments and difficult situations. Now that i think of it, it would seem as though the process of living life, learning from mistakes, healing and growing, well this is the journey toward co-creating and manifesting purpose.

But this is only part of it, right? If what i just described is the part that was set into motion after birth, what was the part of it that you brought into this world? What are the ancestral memories that you carry and what are their implications for my/our life's purpose?

Indeed i have many questions about purpose and meaning, and yet as they form here on the page i feel your wise presence gently reminding me that part of the beauty of life is in the journey of discovery. Along the way we (in this body community) are given cues that affirm we are making decisions and behaving in ways that are aligned with the spiritual aspect of purpose that you carry. We are also offered guidance by other people, experiences (even very difficult ones), observations and the natural world, including plant and animal relatives, the sacred lands and waters, and more.

I think, Soul, that this exploration into our life's purpose is a journey of discovery and healing. It is a journey of looking at the experiences we've had—my interpretation of them—especially those which brought me to crossroads and peeling them back like layers of an onion to get to the source experience, the moment in which the negative feelings about myself (self-talk, self-acceptance, self-judgment, worthlessness) and the stories they informed were planted in my subconsciousness. Once at the source, we can offer to one another the healing necessary to fundamentally shift all the unhealthy narratives that were built upon it.

On this journey, i am also reminded of the many beautiful and affirming moments, people, experiences and observations we've had and created. I remember mistakes and lessons. i remember that all of this is connected to purpose.

So how do i know that we are on the right path? As i look back on our life i realize that at various points along the way affirmations, messages and encounters would remind me that there was something bigger happening and that i am a part of it.

Back in '97 while attending Howard University, for example, my housemate at the time held a vision for a women of color festival that would create a space for my participation as one of many coordinators and festival cook. It was humbling to be part of a group of incredible

Black and brown women committed to creating a gathering that was for us and centered creative expression, healing, and joy. Tired after a long day of unloading food from a delivery truck and organizing it in the kitchen space, i leaned up against a support beam on the front porch of the dining hall in Maryland where we held the festival, and took in the beautiful vision of the land before me. I thought about what we were about to do there: create a safe, intergenerational, women of color-only place to experience the magic of one another and experience the magic of nature at this music-healing festival. I knew i was supposed to be there. I knew that we were in the right place, doing the right thing at the right time. I felt in alignment with our divine purpose.

It seems that there are two ways to think about purpose as i revisit the memories in these letters. One is purpose as an overarching theme in life and the other is purpose that emerges while living life, or, in other words, purpose that is defined time and time again as life is lived. When i look back on our life, Soul, i see evidence of both. The overarching theme appears to be in healing across generations, with experiences good, bad, and indifferent providing valuable classrooms for instruction, as uncomfortable, even painful, as this learning was at times. The aspect of purpose that emerges, or is defined, throughout life is realized through various experiences, endeavors, or projects. I know that my actions are purpose aligned, for example, when a certain feeling emerges in our body, like the feeling that comes with having discovered the answer to a question i didn't know i had. That "aha" feeling.

From them, i've been able to learn, for example, that the impacts of trauma in previous generations can be passed to subsequent ones and to break cycles and invite healing, attention, intention, patience, and care are required in relationships. As i've come to learn this, i have noticed that we've held greater compassion and understanding when interacting with others.

Arriving at this understanding over time has required a reimagining and reinterpretation of the various events and experiences we've had, particularly those that caught me off guard or were overwhelming in their presence, leaving me exposed, vulnerable, traumatized at times. It has also helped me to reckon with the role i played in harming others and as best as possible, owning up, apologizing, and making amends. Here i write 'me' and 'i' as opposed to 'we' because you, Soul, feel like the purist part of us. That part that knew all along that we'd make it through, that part that maintained connection with the Ancestors, calling them in when needed. That aspect of us that communicated with our Spirit Guides, sending and receiving messages over the years, aligning my steps with the direction that would lead to fulfillment of my purposes and destiny.

Equipped with the near pristine vision of hindsight and appreciation for the understanding that we chose to be born, i can view traumatic, harmful, disappointing experiences as teachers. Teachers who have something to show me about myself, about the world, about others. To be clear, Soul, this reframing is for our healing, nourishment, and growth toward fulfillment of our destiny and not to excuse the behavior of anyone else. The men that regarded our body as a toy for their sexual pleasure also had choices. The family members who permitted distance to grow between us had choices. And i too have a choice about what to do with this information. What you told me in your last letter was on point: *we have the power to decide what to do with the experiences we have and information we glean.*

I pay my deepest respects to you, Soul, for keeping us together, not letting us fall apart, remaining connected with Nyame[8], my spirit guides and ancestors and seeking their intervention when needed.

With Gratitude,
    Mind

---

[8] Nyame, in Akom tradition, is the Creator, giver of life.

Mind,

The answers you seek lay within. Notice clues in the meaning of your name. Remember, in the stillness of meditation. Discover evidence in the experiences of life. And listen.

There is so much you alone cannot know. Step back to allow me to be your inner guide.

May your truth be known,
Soul

Reflection Space

Please grab your journal and reflect on the questions, thoughts, words, word sequences and/or images that come to your mind as you reflect on the content of this chapter.

    I offer the following prompts to get you started, if needed: What themes resonate and why? What experiences or encounters taught you something about yourself, life, and/or purpose? What are the recurring themes and lessons in your life? What do they mean to you?

Chapter Four: A Letter to Reader, My Kindred Spirit

Dear Kindred Spirit/Reader,

Knowing if i am on the right path toward fulfillment of my life purpose is something that i am reminded of repeatedly as i open myself to learn and grow from tough times and good, from situations that lend themselves to learning to those that don't, from people to plants, animals, and elements. Indeed, that is much to gain both from the experiences in which i was, or felt, mistreated and those in which i've mistreated or caused harm to others. Neither of these means that i've been off purpose in life, or that somehow my life doesn't have meaning and purpose. On the contrary these are moments that have allowed me to grow in the areas where work was needed but hadn't happened.

There are some issues that have surfaced in different ways and at different times, issues that have served as teachers in various contexts and situations. I've learned about forgiveness, discovered my worth, found my voice, grappled with feeling invisible, struggled with acceptance, and worked through judgment. In various situations, i have been the one who's sought forgiveness for something i'd done, and in others, i've had to find forgiveness in my heart, whether the other person was engaged in that process or not.

Sometimes i wonder if i spend too much time thinking, which potentially takes me away from the experience of cultivating wisdom. Perhaps this is the case. But i'd like to think that for me, there is something in the process of peeling back the layers to understand what i can and pushing the boundaries a bit that is helping to cultivate deeper knowledge and wisdom.

Not all are so mentally-oriented. We are all different. Some, like my sister with whom i was raised—whom i consider to be a very wise person—seems to be a quiet, observer of life, someone who is unassuming and doesn't weigh in on intellectual debates, social issues, or historical opinions; not because she doesn't have opinions, but because there is so much more to life that can be gained by listening and observing. She has a depth of understanding of so many issues and their ethical underpinnings that is incredibly impressive and instructive.

Yet, i am of a disposition to ask questions, even the same ones over and over again at different stages of my life to assess their relevance and meaning in the different moments. Perhaps discovery of my purpose is in investigating the tracks i've left along the way, the work i've already done, the practice of listening to the voice of my heart to stop doing this thing at once so that i can explore this other thing, even if it doesn't seem to make sense at the time.

Ultimately, when I think about understanding and fulfilling purpose, I am drawn to a few key points.

There is an element of purpose that the soul carries into this life that is connected to spirit (the ancestors, Creator, other). And there is an element of purpose that we create along the way. The element of purpose that the soul brings into this world is sometimes revealed by the recurring issues that can assume different forms throughout the course of someone's life. Dealing with what may seem like the same issues over and over allows a person to learn the different aspects of themselves, to be tested on earlier lessons, to learn new things under new conditions and/or at a different stage in one's life to see how far one has grown. When you think you've worked something out, guess what? There is still more to learn from it.

One of the classrooms in which i've spent considerable time has been that of self-love and non-judgment. Learning self-love and acceptance, which i see as being intimately connected, has definitely required work. The homework i've received in this classroom of life has been a combination of:
1. Creating and reciting affirmations
2. Countering negative thoughts that arise in my mind in response to or in the midst of certain situations
3. Diving into the experiences in which the seeds of judgment and lack of love were planted and observing their birth, placing sweetness there and prayers of release, forgiveness and healing.

On this journey of life, we often make mistakes in our efforts to get things right. The mistakes i've made in life have provide opportunities to learn something; something that my ego (expressed as stubbornness, hard headedness) or my experiences, for whatever reason, didn't allow me to understand. I would know that i made a mistake because of the impact of the environment i was in or the people involved, or something within my heart/spirit recognized that i did something wrong in that moment. Mistakes during my life as a human being I liken to failures in the scientific world. Failures—perhaps misnamed—provide important information for the scientist who learns what works and what doesn't work and under what conditions. Like a scientist, we can consider the mistakes we make as valuable sources of information that can be used to support our learning, growth and development. As humans in relation to other humans and beings in the world, we can remember that learning, growth and development is sometimes uncomfortable, painful and may require amends to be made.

Finally, i think fulfilling one's purpose requires listening and doing. These dual practices of listening and doing were beautifully and simply articulated by one of my teachers, who taught that it is not enough to listen to the guidance of my own body, spirit guides, ancestors, and the Creator. Rather it is important to act upon that guidance or what we've learned, mindfully as opposed to blindly; in the service of healing, growing, developing and connecting, as opposed to creating harm; and being open to the ways that this guidance can shift, shape, and facilitate growth in your life. Over time, cultivating the practice of listening has been important on my journey of life; listening to my gut, my intuition, my spirit, my body and then doing something.

What does it mean to listen? There are different ways that our soul communicates, that our spirits speak to ourselves, that our ancestors speak to us. In my experience as an Okomfo, for some (or at certain times), the soul sends a message through the gentle movement of the wind passing between leaves on a tree or the utterances of an unknown person who one may encounter in the course of a day. A message that is embedded in the context of a tv show, conversation or presentation, or experience. It can be subtle or overt.

Whatever it is, there is a way that guidance and messages come to us from our spirit guides and inner soul. Though not the most elegant example, i recall one time when walking to the train station on my way to work. Self-critical thoughts were going through my mind. I was in one of my abusive tangents, calling myself names, beating myself up for not having done something in the way i thought it should've gone. There were many thoughts swirling through my mind. Just as i stepped off the curb to cross the walk, i fell into a crack that i had passed many times before, but somehow missed in this precise moment. I landed on my hands and knees. My bag rolled off my shoulders and fell onto the pavement. Because it was after the early morning rush of school children and workers, only a few people turned their heads as they kept walking to the metro's entrance. Fortunately, there were no laughs that i saw, or i might have felt the need to feign injury to mask embarrassment. As i picked up my body and my ego from the ground, i immediately traced my thoughts back to the moment when I fell to recall what was happening in and around me.

One of the things my Teacher, Nana Ankobiahene Oparebea Bekoe, instructed was to notice the thought that comes in moments when something happens or catches my eyes. In this case, I could've simply fallen because i was deep in thought and didn't pay attention to the curb. In fact, this very thing happened to me in New York several years previously. I was walking to the bookstore in a flood of people crossing the street when I fell right in the middle of the street because I hadn't noticed the hole in front of me.

With the fall at the train station, however, i immediately knew in my gut that there was a message there. It had to do with the way i was talking to myself, the energy i was directing to myself with the negative talk. It was like i was hexing my spirit, sending bad energy to myself with the thoughts going through my mind. This is one example of the way that one's soul, ancestors or spirit guides can show us something. I encourage you to notice the way your spirit guides speak to you and cultivate the practice of noticing what comes to you when certain things happen.

So back to the question, what does it mean to listen? It means hearing what your own spirit (call it gut) and guides are trying to tell you. And so then, the thing to do next is do something about it. Act on the information that comes, where appropriate. Going back to the example when i fell while talking bad to myself. If the message is to recognize the impact of self-hexing on my life and to stop doing that, then the action element is to stop doing it. But what if doing it has become such a habit, that simply ceasing to condemn myself is impossible in and of itself? Or perhaps it is not impossible, but because circumstances that may lead me to condemn myself will come up repeatedly, the doing involves breaking habits over time and creating new ones.

In what part of the body does listening take place? Listening with one's soul or spiritual ear happens in many different ways. Listening can involve reading the signs in nature, hearing what is said or not said from the mouth of another (sometimes the Gods can give us messages through others without their knowing). Or they can put us in the presence of others precisely because they can offer something that our soul needs to hear in a particular moment. And listening is being open to whatever that message is.

Sometimes the receptors for hearing are in your gut, sometimes they are the middle of the head, sometimes they are in the raising of goosebumps. Whispers in the ear. There are many ways and specific ways that a particular individual may hear.

And in the end, i am left with the conclusion that there is life purpose that my soul was given. And the experience of being human provides opportunity to elevate to that, to accomplish that. If it takes more than one lifetime to do it, then i will continue to come back.

Love,
       Afriye

Reflection Space

Please grab your journal and reflect on the questions, thoughts, words, word sequences and/or images that come to your mind as you reflect on the content of this chapter.

I offer the following prompts to get you started, if needed: What themes resonate and why? What classrooms have you spent time in to learn important lessons? How do you hear messages from your soul, ancestors, spirit guides, and/or the Creator?

Chapter Five: Conversations With My Ancestors

we sat together
in that sacred place called home
til' time came to leave

To All My Maternal Ancestors,

Greetings my dear maternal ancestors. I am writing this letter to you in my pursuit for answers to questions my heart has carried for some time, particularly with regard to my life's purpose. As your living descendent, is part of my purpose—or one of my purposes–to help repair, heal or strengthen something in our family lineage?

I am asking this of other ancestors too, but want to start with you because it is your living descendants that cared for me while i was growing up. It wasn't my father's side of the family or anyone else. It was my mama, aunties and their mom, my granny, who did. And, don't let me forget my granddaddy. He and my granny married when both were in their forties and divorced and remarried a few times in the thirty plus years they were together. He loved my granny so much that he gave up alcohol for her, which for an alcoholic is no small feat.

I seek guidance from you first because your living descendants raised me. They showed up to care for me regardless of what they were dealing with in their lives (poverty, heartbreak, depression, sickness, unexpected pregnancy, joy, etc.). Though each generation struggled with its own angels and demons, my granny, aunts, mom, me, and my daughter did the best we could in trying to do better than the generation before. To me this says something about you, about the spirit of this lineage, about resilience, survival, and intention (or perhaps hope) to get better, whatever that means, i.e., healing, repairing, evolving, growing.

I seek guidance from you first because i want to recognize your place in my life. I want to honor the lives you lived; lives that made possible the conditions for my existence. I wish i were able to remember you more clearly, vividly.

I wonder if before my soul made the journey to join with the growing embryo in my mother's body, we sat together in the Land of the Nsamando[9] attending to the needs of our human relatives, engaging in meaningful spiritual activities, and sharing lessons accrued over many lifetimes. I wonder if our souls played a role in bringing elevation and light into the various realms of consciousness, battled the forces of darkness or engaged in other divine spiritual activities. Or did we perhaps reside separate from one another, in different spaces and places according to the specific level of attainment of our destinies?

In writing this letter to you as my maternal

---

[9] This is the land of the ancestors in the spiritual tradition of Akom.

ancestors, i recognize that you represent many ancestral lineages, each with powerful stories of emergence and movement, opportunities and challenges, aging, sickness (perhaps), and death. On my granny's side, you are the Nichols, Workoffs (Workuff?) and Hardings. On my biological grandfather's side you are the Flemings and Rosses. And, of course, the Garlins; my granddaddy's people who though not related by blood, are connected in spirit, through the care and devotion he showed to my granny. In your diversity and sameness, you live within me.

I want to let you know that i have re-written this letter many times. In earlier versions, i expressed deep frustration about the absence of the men in our family for what i speculated went on for generations based upon what i witnessed in my lifetime. For example, in an earlier version of this letter i wrote:

> What was it that passed from one generation to the next, seemingly leaving the men in our family sickened with the disease of absence? Spurred, perhaps by the pain of childhood that was never resolved, leaving distance as the only comfort-provided? Perhaps too the social and material conditions of existence exerted such pressure on your families that separation provided the only avenue for survival.

But as i wrote, Mary Ross, my mother's paternal great-great-grandmother, paid me a visit in a dream. Did you all know she came right in and called me out? In my mind's eye, Mother Mary imprinted a very clear and curt message: *don't interpret our lives through the narrow experience of yours.* These weren't her exact words, but this is my best summation. This ancestor, who prior to this moment was simply a name on my family tree, let me know in no uncertain terms that not only was she (and we) so much more, but i needed to sit my behind down and humbly listen, study, and learn what you may be willing to share with me about my life's purpose, while refraining from making assumptions about theirs. It seemed as though so many of you lined up behind her in support of her guiding admonition.

So here i am. Humbly ready to sit my behind down and listen. I want to listen to what you have to say about what my charge is in relation to our lineage. I am thinking that it has something to do with ancestral healing. But i ask you, does it?

With gratitude,
        Your Daughter

Poem To My Ancestors

with you
i have shared so much
from you
i want to learn
in the stillness of this moment
i listen

Dear Mother Mary,

I've been sitting with the message you sent me in my dream. Do you remember? Do you remember that you called on me to dig deeper, take the time to learn through study and reflection (also listening) and challenge the assumptions i hold about our family, the men in particular, that informed the lens through which i saw you all?

The experiences i've had in my life and the observations i've made about my mom's generation and her parents' generation are valuable but should not serve as the basis for drawing conclusions about previous generations, nor for fully comprehending the dynamics that pass from one generation to the next. As i was growing up, for example, i noticed and developed judgments around the hard stuff, like watching my mom struggle economically to raise a growing brood of children, on her own. As the eldest child, i saw her seeking love in relationships with men who never stayed. I made similar observations about my granny and feared the same outcome for myself: multiple children from different fathers, loneliness, poverty, and cycles of depression. I concluded, in my young mind, that these dynamics passed from one generation to the next and that men stay around long enough to make babies and extract labor and resources from women, but they don't stay around long enough to take care of the children or work on relationships. I wondered how far back these dynamics went, but not having access to family history or really anything more than the names of relatives on a family tree, i assumed that the men in our family have always been like this. Your message suggested otherwise.

Your message challenged me to remember that even in my own life, some men were doing things differently. For example, my youngest brother's father remained in his life, and to this day they are close. My granddaddy married and remarried my granny multiple times, ultimately giving up alcohol permanently for her to take him back.

You also drew me to memories i had taken for granted of expressions of resilience, creativity, joy, and excellence in my family. I remembered that my granny and mom used to always correct me when i spoke slang around them or ended sentences with prepositions because they thought that by talking what they considered "proper" would give me a chance to get an education and make it in this world. It drove me up the wall, but i am certain that it helped me to be a stronger writer as it reinforced at home the grammar lessons i learned in school.

I remembered my granny's collection of *National*

Geographic magazines from as far back as the late 60s because it was her way of traveling the world. In me, she inspired a desire to learn about peoples and places far beyond the small spaces of Detroit, Ann Arbor, and Toledo. I remember my granny crocheted each of her grandchildren a beautiful bed covering because, besides her physical presence in our lives, that was one thing that she could give of herself to us. That care and tenderness that went into creating the perfect floral squares, delicately woven together into a beautiful tapestry of reds and purples, delighted my senses and showed me that there were different ways to demonstrate love beyond saying the words "i love you," which she never did. There are so many more examples i can share, but what i want to appreciate is that as much as painful, hard dynamics can be reproduced from one generation to the next, so too can supportive, joyful ones be passed down.

What is also coming to my mind as i write this is that sometimes people's life choices and lives diverge from those of previous generations, which means that the people and lives i've been able to observe in my short time on this earth may be different from how you, your parents, and your children lived; and it may be different from how you have wanted them to live. I know beautiful, open people who were born to incredibly strict, dogmatic parents; i have seen people mistreated by parents who were also mistreated, yet grow up to be kind, sensitive, and determined to break the cycles of abuse; i have seen parents pour their best into a child only for the grips of drug use or violence to seize them. So much can change in one generation. So i appreciate you calling me on the carpet for that.

Your encouragement of me to challenge my assumptions about the men in your family line, pushes me to think differently about my granny's lineage and affirms for me the need for ancestral healing because somewhere something became broken. However you might have lived your life, Mother Mary, somewhere in the five generations between you and i, something changed enough for me to have seen absence, violence, pent up anger, depression, and struggle in two of them. While i don't have the capacity, nor do i think that as one person i can do everything, there are some things i can do, such as healing with my mom and daughter. And maybe, just maybe, positive impacts could be passed down to those yet to come and passed up to you who reside in the *Land of the Nsamando*.[10]

For several years, my daughter Nia has initiated the work of healing between my mother and me through courageous conversations. Though difficult at times, those conversations have helped us to become closer and understand each other better. More formally, in the fall of 2020 i became inspired to embark on a project of healing between my mom, daughter, and me. The inspiration came while i was on a journey begun in June of that year, a journey whose purpose was to support healing between

---

[10] Place where the Nsamanfo, or ancestors, reside.

Black and Indigenous/Native people, across generations, with the Mississippi River as witness and guide. As we began the journey from the river's headwaters, i became curious about what healing across generations in my own family might look like and what the implications for those born before and after us might be.

Mother Mary, with the information i had at the time and the assumptions about the generations before me i held in my heart, as well as my own experiences, i went into this project with a three-fold intention: to break harmful cycles, heal the wounds, and create conditions that facilitate and support continued health and wellbeing. I wrote up my greatest hopes for this project and want to share it with you here:

> In doing this work, I aspire to fulfill one of my central purposes in life: facilitating healing in my family line. And my greatest hope is that in the course of interviewing my mother, daughter and granddaughter, as well as reflecting on my own parenting and experiences as a daughter, we can affirm the beautiful contributions to our daughter's lives, as well as surface harmful cycles that have found their way across generation in spite of our best efforts. And understand what fuels them and how we can support one another in ending their unwelcome presence in our lives. It is also my hope that in this process we can heal and strengthen our relationships in ways that not only impact those of us who are living, but also those who

have come and will one day return.

Together we explored several questions, including: What were some of the things your parents did that you experienced as positive, experiences you wanted to embody in your own parenting? What were some of the things your parents did that you experienced as hurtful, harmful and/or that you didn't want to include in your own parenting? I also asked them to think about the impact of how they were parented on who they are now (or have been as an adult) and to reflect upon the practices/experiences that affirmed who they were as a person and those that left scars and/or have required healing.

These conversations were hard for me, for all of us, but helpful, even healing. Nia expressed in an email what she held in her heart, and we were able to talk about it. In preparation for our first Q&A session, she wrote:

> Watching my mother appear powerless was harmful. I had learned that my mother married out of respect for someone, to ground herself, and to create some type of stability for her child. However, what I actually had observed and internalized was that my mother silently suffered as a man I had never known took full control over her life as well as her daughters. I perceived that neither one of our voices mattered and that was very harmful for me to internalize during a major time in my life. I believe it is crucial to include children in major life changes such as marriage, moving, etc. But oftentimes

> children learn that their parents' desires are more important, and we just have to learn how to keep going and adapt.

I read this with an open heart and, admittedly, with a bit of defensiveness and regret. I think she wrote to me in the third person because this was as hard for her to articulate as it was for me to hear. I had made decisions that impacted her life in major ways. But isn't that what parents do? She made me think about how my mom also moved my siblings and i around a lot and married a man who was not good as a husband to my mom or stepfather to me, but was good to my brothers, including his son. Children never have choices in these matters, i thought, because parents have their reasons for doing things. But what a difference might it have made in me or in our relationship had my thoughts and feelings been considered by my mom in her decisions? Might there have been a different in the relationship with my daughter, had i considered her thoughts and feelings?

My daughter asked for my responses to her answers to my questions. She wanted to know what my version of events was, particularly those that were painful, so she could more deeply understand the surrounding circumstances, process them holistically and continue her and our healing together. In response to what she said, i wrote the following:

> I wasn't powerless. I made choices, even when they caused me great pain, sadness or sent me in spirals of depression. I just wanted

> stability for you in your life and thought that i was with a person that could create that. What i didn't realize was that the kind of stability offered would require that i stifle the creative fires that burned within me. I thought i was doing the best i could. As you will undoubtedly believe you are doing with Phoenix. Each generation we are trying to do better, as i certainly see you doing with her.

With my mom, i listened deeply, asked questions and took notes. We didn't have this kind of exchange. My mom is in her seventies, and it seemed that her memory of parenting of me had been revised a bit. I couldn't bear to contradict the ways she said she said she fostered openness with me, listened to me, encouraged me to come to her about sexual abuse. "I don't know why you didn't think you could come to me," she said. Her words stung as i thought about how emotionally unavailable she was to me coming up. But understandably so, as she had a lot on her plate, between raising five children, trying to make ends meet financially, and dealing with her own feelings and realities. In other ways her parenting intentions were largely seen. She did, for example, not talk bad about my dad in front of me or beat me when i wet the bed; both things that happened to her as a child. I know that she did her best to raise my siblings and me with little help from the fathers. Mom carried a lot, and i am so grateful for her tenacity and resilience.

Mother Mary, i don't know if this work with my mom and daughter is the pathway of healing across generations, but something in the conversations with them suggests that we are headed in the right direction. We are beginning to see one another in our humanity a bit more.

I do, however, need to take initiative to respond to the questions i asked them. I realize that i didn't answer the questions i asked mom and Nia for myself, nor did they ask me to either. How do i feel about that? I don't know. An attempt to answer brings up things i struggle with admitting to myself. With my daughter, i want to cultivate a level of openness that felt unattainable with my mom, openness that accompanies a high degree of trust, support, affection and love. Indeed, this is happening by having these kinds of courageous conversations, by listening to one another, spending time with one another, and sharing what is happening in our lives. And when curiosity brings forth questions, i answer, we engage and explore together.

With my mom, however, it is different. The things i want to express get trapped in my throat because i don't want to cause her pain at this stage in her life. I don't want her to feel guilty about anything. And i don't want to feel ashamed, be shamed, or get cut off from further conversation because of an inability or unwillingness to really hear things from my perspective. Plus, as the eldest of her children with the benefit of accompanying her through so much of her life, i know that she did her best. So, composting the emotions that have resulted from feeling unprotected by her at key stages in my early life and feeling as though she was emotionally unavailable to me, has been an important part of my healing and growth. She was only a teenager when she began having children and had to find a way to get by with what she had.

It seems that somewhere in all of this is the formula for healing both within each of us and in relation to one another, *across generations,* and serves as a critical element in ancestral healing given our previous and future tenure as ancestors. Through our willingness to get to know one another, be vulnerable together and have honest, even difficult conversations, our understanding grows, compassion deepens, and we learn about forgiveness and releasing or transforming the blame and pain. This work shifts the dynamics between us, the dynamics that pass to and through our descendants and what we carry with us into the spirit world when we die. Since this work, for example, my daughter and i have gotten much closer and in some ways, my mom has begun to be more open with me. The work is ongoing, through the love remains ever present.

With humble gratitude,
      Your Great Great Great Granddaughter

May We Heal

I remember you
I remember you in me
I remember me in you
I remember me

I love you
I love you in me
I love me in you
I love me

I forgive you
I forgive you in me
I forgive me in you
I forgive me

I honor you
I honor you in me
I honor me in you
I honor you

May those yet to come be blessed by our healing

Dear Mother Eula,

Warm greetings to you. I am writing you with a bit of trepidation. The few stories i heard about you cast you as a cold, uncaring mother who favored your second born over my granny and who lived in the same house as your grandchildren (my mom, aunts, and uncles), but never spoke a word to them. What were the circumstances in your life that led to this kind of expression of motherhood and grandparenthood? I wonder if a more loving approach might have given my granny better tools to cope with motherhood and the myriad burdens she carried throughout her life. And with better tools, i wonder if she might have been able to have greater love, patience and compassion for her children. Might my uncles have turned out differently?

Looking at my uncles' lives through the lens of my experiences, it appeared that within my two maternal uncles grew a form of sinister disdain for women over the years. The hate they held for women would lead to venomous verbal attacks on their mother until she ceased taking their calls. Throughout one uncle's late forties and fifties, he would curse her out for being a bad mother and blame her for all that was wrong in his life. His preoccupation with blaming her, physically and emotionally abusing his girlfriend, and feeling sorry for himself seemed more important to him than raising and caring for his own daughter, who grew up without him.

The other uncle expressed his disdain for women in the snatching of the lives of his most intimate relationships. I remember the first woman he killed. Tinashe[11] was her African name—*may she rest in peace and power.* She was a police officer. I remember her kindness and beauty. Tinashe sported a large, neatly coiffed afro and had big brown eyes and smooth chocolate

---

[11] A pseudonym of Shona origin that means "God is with us."

skin. What i remember most about Tinashe was that music seemed to follow her when she walked. That soulful blend of Earth, Wind and Fire and Marvin Gaye. Uncle's brutal act weighed heavy on our family, generating a kind of persistent grief, loss and sadness that dug its claws onto the edges of our hearts.

The low regard my uncles seemed to have for women, expressed through their actions, stemmed from difficult childhoods, and complicated, pain-filled relationships with their mother, my granny. The painful upbringing was shared by their women siblings, including my mom whose childhood continues to surface feelings that trigger emotional reactions even in her seventies. But how and why was it that her and my aunts didn't express violence in the ways the men did?

As a child coming up witnessing some of the behaviors of the men in my life, it seemed as though they made messes that the women persistently cleaned up and they left children for the women to raise. Additionally, the bonds between the women were strong, even as they were tainted with bitterness toward their mother and with one another at times. It was these women, however, whom i witnessed trying to break the cycles of abuse that they inherited as best as they could. Though their children might put forward their own criticisms about the parenting they received from their seniors, objectively it can be said that they/we weren't abused to the extent that our mothers were.

And if i were to look at the life of Granny, a woman

with whom i had a special relationship, she was very different with her grandchildren than she was with her own offspring. She cared for us in ways that she was unable to care for her own children. As the relationship with my mom's father soured and Granny was left to raise five young children on her own, i wonder what forms of rejection and hurdles she encountered as a single, poor Black woman in the late 1940s and 1950s.

The stress and pressure she held within her body must've been considerable, as she had a nervous breakdown when her children were all under seven. My Aunt Marie (whom we were blessed to have as a family friend) told me one morning Granny came to her house behaving nervously, jittery—a little frantic. Aunt Marie asked, "What happened? What's going on?" And Granny began crying. Through her tears she said that she put the children on the bus to the state orphanage. Somehow the pain, the pressure, the conditions of her life were too great and the only support she was able to get came from a system that at that time sought to keep Black families apart.

Clearly the relationship between her only sister and you, Mother Eula, didn't allow her to consider you all as options, leaving this as the only one. The children remained in an orphanage long enough for the state to find other family members to take them in. It was then that they moved to Kentucky to stay with the paternal grandparents of three of the children.

Recall that the Flemings had at that time lived in

Lexington, Kentucky, for several generations. For two years, my mom and her siblings lived with these grandparents. And for these same two years, Granny fought to get her children back. According to Aunt Marie (because Granny never spoke about her life, as many didn't from that generation), Granny almost immediately began the fight to get her children back but ran into one obstacle after another because of the compounding impacts of poverty, race, and gender; she just wasn't deemed fit to care for her children and was repeatedly reminded about that. But alas, she persisted and was finally able to bring them home.

Two years to a child can feel like a lifetime. And the justifiable confusion, sadness and anger her children felt toward her for having been given up (or in their minds, tossed away) was met with pain and trauma expressed as anger from their mother. From this one source experience sprung forth relationship dynamics that would play out over the years as deep bitterness and division, emotional and physical abuse, moments of joy and laughter tainted by the ever presence of fear, loneliness, and cycles of depression. My mom was so deeply impacted that even in her early seventies, she grapples with the lasting impacts of her early life.

What i've been able to understand about Granny's life was that she had a very strained relationship with you, Mother Eula. When my mother and her siblings were children they lived in the same house as you, but you never spoke to them, according to my mother's recollection.

What kind of impact must that have had on Granny as a young, single mother who needed your support? In what ways did that impact how she showed up with her own children?

I imagine that parenting must have been tough for you, too. A records search indicated that you were widowed when your girls were young. I remember discovering death certificates of the twin boys you gave birth to before my granny and her sister were born; both died in their infancy. What other realities and feelings were you dealing with? What was your life like?

Mother Eula, i am seeing more clearly the healing across generations and ancestral healing scope of work. It involves multiple lineages because each has its own set of issues. By engaging with my mom, i am calling forth her mother–granny–and her mother before that–you–and so on to step forward and join us. If this is as far as i get in sending love, compassion, and grace to you three, i know that something important has begun, as i already see in the dynamics my daughter is co-creating with her daughter.

With tenderness,
    Your Great Granddaughter

Healing's Ebbs and Flows

a force lurking in the shadows
moving into my body and taking up space
a void left by injury
filled

a member advising me to find solace in passions deferred
reminding me that to walk across that threshold brings
pain
exposures that lead only to
trauma

a memory of the erasure of hard work and good intention
tarnishing my good name and legacy
nothing good exists beyond these
walls

a shrinking space that has become my world
challenging to stand, i can only hunch
a disquieting existence, uncomfortable, achy
disfiguring

gentle admonitions by ancestors to not forget why
flashing images of purpose in my mind's eye
a reminder that traumas are teachers too

calls by my Guides to get up and stand tall
facing the fears that have left me crippled
a call to repair and heal and learn

i stand. i shatter. i learn. i repair. i grow.

i question. i doubt. i worry. i doubt. i shrink.

a force lurking in the shadows returns
revisiting familiar places
resuming its work
repeating old tropes
following familiar paths
poisoning my movement
crippling my growth
undoing everything

Letter to the Ancestors of My Acquired Father's Lineage

Dear Grandma and Grandpa,

Up until about a year ago, there was so much i wanted to say to you—so much i wanted to ask. At an earlier stage in life, my questions would've been tinged with anger, frustration, and sadness at the lingering pain of rejection i felt from you both when you were alive, as well as your daughters/my aunts. I would have loved to direct some of my anger at my dad too, but as you know, at such a young age in my life his mental condition deteriorated so rapidly i don't recall ever being able to hold a conversation with him. Where do those feelings of anger and frustration go with a person incapable of sustained verbal communication?

Admittedly using familial words such as dad, aunt, grandma, and grandpa feels hard. Though accurate in that they identify the nature of our connection with one another, these monikers feel disingenuous for the closeness of relationships they suggest. I simply don't feel close or connected with you all. But alas, we are here.

I believe part of the work of ancestral healing is for leaning into the places that are uncomfortable, hard, and unknown. You knowing that your son claimed me as his child was uncomfortable for you and you rejected that, going so far as to take the issue up with the courts. I found these documents when poking around in some of my mom's stacks of papers as a teenager. The judge threw the case out because your son signed my birth certificate. Reading those papers provided evidence of the rejection i felt coming from you during my summer visits as a youth; rejection in the form of cool distance and few words.

To be fair, you were responsible for a few enduring positive memories i've had about my childhood. It was during those couple of summer visits my sister and i spent with you that i freely wandered in the woods adjacent to your house in Michigan, exploring the communities of mushrooms, mosses, and bugs busily moving amongst the fallen branches and trees. I remember the moist woody scented air in the days following heavy rains. It was also during these visits that i saw the value of growing one's own food as Grandma daily tended to your abundant garden of root and leafy vegetables, tomatoes, and more. I enjoyed home cooked meals featuring garden delights and baked goods, such as dinner rolls, salads, and pastas.

I watched you, Grandma, pick cabbage, tomatoes, and squash from the garden and weave them into fresh tasting meals, which was so different from the processed foods i was used to eating in the welfare boxes we got from the government. There weren't fresh veggies in these boxes, rather highly processed cheeses, milks, cereals and canned foods full of salt. These experiences of you in your garden, and the foods you brought to the table, created more than fond memories; they were foundational to who i am today as a gardener, earth advocate, and tree relative. The soil and trees are where i go for comfort, healing, and connection.

I wonder how much these positive memories tempered the impact of the distance i felt when visiting. Neither of you spoke much to me or around me, and mealtime conversations largely consisted of my own chattiness and questions. I wondered why you didn't talk with me the way you seemed to talk with your other grandchildren. Was it because your son and my mom didn't stay together? Did you blame my mom for your son's rapid descent into paranoid schizophrenia, which rendered him incapable of holding conversations and caring for himself? Did you think my sister and i might by extension be to blame?

Perhaps my greatest fears were confirmed that fateful summer of 2005 when going into my freshman year of high school my mom received a call from Aunt H, saying that my sister and i couldn't visit. Perhaps in her unwillingness to be the bearer of bad news, my mom handed me the phone so Aunt could tell me directly. When i got on the phone, Aunt H said that they just didn't have enough money to take us shopping this time and maybe next year things would be better. *Why did she think that we needed to go shopping?* i wondered. I pled with her. "Aunt, we don't need to go shopping; you don't have to buy us anything. We just want to see dad. We want to see you." She apologized and said that she had to go. My efforts were in vain. I wouldn't see or hear from any of you for another twenty-five years.

It also happened that in that same year i stumbled

across the court documents i mentioned earlier. Your attempts, Grandma, to dispute my dad's paternity of me (whose skin is brown), but curiously not my sister (whose skin is much lighter), led my teenage mind to conclude that you—and by extension your entire family—rejected me as the Black child of her white son. Did you know that i tried to take my life shortly after reading all of that?

I don't want to tell you, but i will, that at thirteen years old, the pain of your rejection intensified the heaviness i already carried from the impacts of sexual abuse, bullying, and seeing my mom struggle so hard to care for all of us kids. I just couldn't bear staying around another day. I am telling you this not to elicit some sort of sympathy. Rather you need to know the impact your behavior had on an innocent child. If dad signed my birth certificate, if he claimed me, why didn't you support him? Why did you fight it and make me feel like i didn't belong?

Early last year[12] i learned what you seem to have suspected all of this time: i am not your biological grandchild. And although there were moments when i suspected this was the case, which i will get into momentarily, a couple of years ago i began to think about what it might look like to reach out to your living relatives and begin building a relationship.

My desire to initiate a healing process with you and your children, my aunts, was seeded some time ago. It began with my cousin inviting me sometime around 2013

---

[12] This letter was written in 2021.

to join and support her as she laid her son (who as you recall was tragically killed in a car accident) to rest on family land in Michigan's Upper Peninsula. In all the years i had been on this earth and been in your lives, this was the first time i was invited to the family land. Though the ferry ride with my sister and her family from the mainland to the island was beautiful—waves lapping the side of the boat, wind whipping my hair in a frenzy, sun beaming on my face—i couldn't enjoy it because of a growing pain in my heart as these old questions that i thought i had laid to rest circulated in my mind: Why was i never invited to visit? Why didn't you see me as good enough to be in your family? Why did you not want me?

I don't recall many things about that visit, but i do remember that it was the first time in twenty-five years that i had laid eyes on you, dad, and other family members. Though i was treated respectfully, there was an air of awkwardness as i was as unknown to you all as you all were to me. I felt like a stranger moving through spaces that might have been familiar had you not pushed me so far away and found comfort at the group's edges where i could see everyone, while being as unseen as i could.

I observed at a distance sincere and touching conversations take place between people who've known one another for years, attended one another's birthdays, celebrated holidays together, and know the names of one another's children. Had our relationship been continuous, i might have sat among them, laughing, reminiscing, sharing in the sadness of a young life cut short. But it wasn't. We didn't know one another. It was what it was, and time creates space for a lot of things to happen. For me, this involved releasing the lingering impacts of pain, rejection and longing for a relationship that never existed. I craved a fantasy of something i wanted, but wasn't based in reality.

Letting go of this longing was so liberating.

Just a few months ago, one of my aunts reached out to me on facebook with a touching message that she would like to get to know me. Another sent a message through my sister that they would love to see me at the family reunion next year. These invitations for connection coming at this stage in my life were welcomed, particularly as i am zeroing in on matters of life purpose and ancestral healing. Perhaps we may now slowly get to know one another. Perhaps we may begin to heal. But not even a full week had passed after receiving the family reunion invitation when i received the DNA results confirming that i am not your blood descendant.

Years ago[13] when i was younger and working to heal the pain in my heart from your rejection of me, i began to question if we were in fact related by blood. At the time i was well into my training as an Okomfo[14] in Akom, an Indigenous spiritual system from West Africa. During this process of intense spiritual development, study and practice, many wounds were being forced open,

---

[13] This was in 2000.

[14] Spiritual healer/priestess

insecurities surfaced, and skeletons exposed to allow for release, healing, and growth. And among the scars were the feelings of rejection that grew from the earlier experiences with your descendants. The journey to becoming a spiritual healer required that i not only work through old and accumulated stuff, but also acquire the tools to continue this work for myself and with others for the remainder of my life. But to say this was difficult would be an understatement.

By my second year of training, the anger and sadness i carried from your rejection of me and all it had come to mean to me grew into yoke that hung heavy around my neck: white folks who couldn't work through their racism to accept their own child, middle class people who thought we wanted you to give us impoverished kids things, a child without a father. Seeing this energy around me one day after making prayers, my Teacher and Godmother, Nana Ankobiahene Oparebea Bekoe challenged me to re-frame what all of this meant for me. For one, she urged me to consider that society tells us families *should* look certain ways, specifically that the nuclear family—heterosexual, cis-gendered mother and father in the home—is the norm and families that are composed differently, even where rejection and abandonment are involved, are wrong, inadequate and lacking. But if i never had a father, then what was i missing? If for years i didn't have his family in my life, might i be willing to release the longing and embrace who is in my life and who has been there the entire time?

Nana Oparebea Bekoe also encouraged me to remember that people are who they are. And they let you know who they are through their actions. These words led me to think long and hard about what this reframing meant for the anger and sadness i carried that on the one hand weighed me down, but on the other provided a sense of protection and comfort from the pain of rejection. It was easier for me to direct my negative emotions toward you all than feel the pain in my heart. It was easier to regard you, your descendants, even your entire lineage, as offspring of the white populations that invaded and colonized nations, raped, murdered, and enslaved African and Indigenous peoples the world over and destroyed lands for profit than to release the anger. Though at some point in history, some of you may have done these things, i was being asked by my teacher at this stage in my spiritual development to let go of the weight, excavate the pain anchored deep in my spirit, and allow for deep healing to happen. Though it would take some time to fully heal, the work began.

It was during this time that i began to wonder if i even were your blood relative. The thoughts initially emerged from an early stage in the healing process when i wanted to reject you as i had been rejected. It took the form of: i won't claim you because you won't claim me. But as the healing work continued, something shifted. I remember feeling the pivot while on a trip to Ghana as part of my Okomfo training. Something opened up within me between hauling water each day and tending to household chores to engaging in sacred ritual and participating in traditions passed down for generations. But it was when i kneeled before my teacher to receive the traditional Okomfo markings that i first felt your son might not be my biological father.

I remember sitting on the floor with others in a simple room filled with pots, ritual objects, burning candles and incense. I wore a single white piece of fabric, secured by a string around my waist and one around my chest. Though it was midday, the room was slightly dim because there were no windows, and the door was cracked. I whispered prayers of gratitude for being here as feelings of anticipation, excitement, and trepidation of receiving my markings filled my body. My teacher called me to kneel before her to begin. I closed my eyes and as she began to mark my body, i immediately saw the words, *you come from someone else.*

When i returned from Ghana, i asked my mom if there might be a chance that your son wasn't my biological father. After a long pause she said yes. We talked for a while, and she gave me the name of the only other person it could be. I spent a few weeks looking the person up and trying to learn more by reaching out to folks who may know something, but nothing ever came of it. So, i dropped all efforts and went on with my life.

With the passage of time my priorities shifted, and attention turned to the realities of my life and life's work. But perhaps it was just a matter of time before my attention would return to you all. It was a matter of time before my spiritual path would lead me to explore how i might facilitate ancestral healing of my family. Though we are unrelated by blood, circumstances brought us together in the spirit. Somewhere in your son's act of claiming me while his mind was lucid and determined, we were connected. Was it your ancestors who guided him to wholly embrace a woman who was already pregnant at the dawn of their relationship? Did he know and never tell? Or did he never know? Whatever the case may be, we are connected for reasons i would like to understand better so that my work with the ancestors—all of my ancestors, blood and spirit—is better informed.

I am curious, what, if any, ancestral work might be necessary as a result of our connection? For years, i have carried deep pain of not having a father and feeling rejected by his family, including you two, for being Black, poor, and the daughter of a woman whom you didn't accept. For years, i sought acceptance from other people for whom i felt i had to shift and change myself just to gain acceptance, otherwise face rejection. So many years wasted with this dance, when self-acceptance was there as an answer the whole time, i was just unable to see it.

What was it that your generations of whiteness needed to learn, experience, or heal by having a Black spiritual offspring in this moment of history? Though you both can rest assured in the spirit world that i am not your biological granddaughter, you were presented with the possibility of having me in your lives and yet chose a course of action that led to a rejection of me. Was it that you were given the opportunity to elevate yourselves with regard to race and/or race relations, but chose not to? What learning remains for you in the ancestral realm and, if any, are you willing to put in this kind of work?

I ask myself the same hard questions: What are the lessons for me? For many years, i wouldn't admit that i had a white father or white family, largely because i didn't feel as though your descendants considered me family. I saw their rejection of me as evidence of their racism (a disease that i could easily understand given the role that whites have played in history) and i didn't want any part of them. Indeed, i resented that white blood ran through my veins knowing how destructive many in your race have been to the Indigenous peoples of the world, as well as to the earth and many ecosystems and biospheres that live within her. It pained me that perhaps somewhere in my ancestry were people who perpetuated destruction and benefited from the myriad systems of oppression erected to bolster your race's unjust rule.

But the resentment that grew within me wasn't only leveled at you and your race, but also at myself for having you and your race in me. The journey to self-acceptance after the seed of rejection was planted early has been long and difficult. Perhaps somewhere in all of this is an important lesson for me; one that could have only been born from the intersection of our spiritual paths.

I don't yet know where this will all lead. But as an Okomfo with a purpose that includes ancestral healing of my blood and spiritual ancestors, i am committed to doing all i can so that the road of my descendants may be guarded by a coterie of Nananom dedicated to assisting them to define and carry out their life purpose.

May we journey well together,
    Afriye

Nsamanfo Terris

Alas you came
to claim
your child.
Thats so wild.
And after all this time.

Letters to My Biological Paternal Ancestors

Dear Biological Paternal Ancestors,

I am not quite sure where to begin this letter. For so long, i longed to know your living relatives, my father especially, even before i truly knew that you all existed. I wanted to see myself reflected in the faces and in the ways of a family, the many parts of me that remained unexplained by my mom's family. And after efforts that led me into dead ends, i gave up, resolving in my heart that these answers weren't for me at this time. I was okay with that.

I signed up for ancestry.com to gain a better understanding of my mother's relatives, to learn who they were, where they came from and anything else i could glean from the results of this search. My interest grew out of the conversations my mom, daughter and i began a couple of years ago about our lives, with hopes and intentions for intergenerational healing. It also grew within a broader journey i was on, the Sacred Waters Pilgrimage, whose purpose was to hold prayers of healing for the

Mississippi River and between Black and Native/Indigenous people in the past, present and future.

The Sacred Waters Pilgrimage began on the summer solstice in 2020. A group of Black and Native/Indigenous women and two-spirit people opened this journey in ceremony at the Mississippi headwaters, continued at 5 locations along this great river on full moons, and ended on the winter solstice where she opens into the Gulf. Seven months of ceremony, prayer, and working with earth-spirit medicines and the chakras left me simultaneously energized, exhausted, vulnerable, exposed, beat up and healed. And, importantly, on that journey i was reminded that what i was doing with and for Black and Native/Indigenous relations—past, present, and future—i too must do within my own family.

I bought the test kit and sent it in.

Imagine my surprise when i received the results and saw confirmed that i am a living descendent of you all and not the people whose name is on my birth certificate.

Did all this spiritual and healing work lay the basis for your showing up in my life at this time?

Curious and trying to be open,
    Your child

There is meaning in all
That we experience
If only we have the eyes to see
The ears to hear
The heart to feel

Dear Enoch,

You decided to leave before we had the opportunity to meet, but your imprint on me is substantial, as hard as it was for me to admit around the time of your passing. Substantial, because of what i've learned about you thus far is that i am so much like you. Like you, i am deeply spiritual, a lover of nature, and an advocate for justice. At the memorial, these words were used to describe you:

> He laughed easily and always had jokes. He loved people, was creative, smart and strong. He loved to discuss theories on life, afterlife, space and time. His spiritual life ran deep, and he spoke about God often. He was kind and considerate to everyone he encountered. He adored nature and loved being among plants and animals, hiking and camping. A lover of music, he played guitar and piano and always sang. He will be missed.[15]

Within your family—in this and in the ancestral worlds—i find all aspects of who i am: what has been noted above, as well as artistic, philosophical and intellectual interests, curiosities, and expressions.

But why this felt hard for me to admit is because i didn't want to be so much like someone who, when told

---

[15] Written by Chelsea Terris Scott and Sara Terris Jones.

that i existed by one of your sisters, denied the possibility. This raw, human emotion that i felt came from a place in me that didn't care that you had been living with schizophrenia all of your adult life, was living in a residential facility at the time due to the level of physical and mental support you needed, and may or may not had been lucid enough to consider the information told to you about me.

What i felt lived within a part of me that remembered the pain of rejection from family members that were supposed to embrace, love, and accept their children and affirm their existence. Your statement in response to the news of me (as told to me by your sister)—*That's not possible*—reopened wounds i thought i had healed.

Given that one of my charges in this life is ancestral healing, i noticed myself asking Nyame questions around the time of your passing that came from this place of pain: Why do i have to pray for the safe journey of a person that denied me? Why do i now have to work with a lineage of ancestors who decided to show up when i was writing a book about purpose that involved ancestral conversations and healing? Why does Enoch and his ancestors get a place in my life (and book), alongside those who have been with me—and who never denied me—all my life?

The answers to these questions came as i acknowledged the pain and challenged myself to move through it. The bottom line is that this is the work i signed up for in this lifetime.

Though we didn't share the same spiritual tradition, i felt called to hold certain rituals for your spirit on a schedule that coincided with my spiritual system. After learning about your passing this past July, i planned to make offerings to Nana Esi[16] and pray for your safe passage in the spirit world on the 40th day of your transition. When that day came, i found that i couldn't do it because i noticed a feeling of resentment in my heart that remained from the sting of rejection.

It took another four months before i was able to compost these feelings into a kind of nourishing energy that readied me to work with you, and by extension, those who came before you. What this looks like now is simple: a monthly greeting, acknowledgement of you, and prayer for you.

After a year, which is when, according to my spiritual tradition, the traveling spirit will have reached the Land of the Nsamando and is ready to work for family members, we shall see what comes next. What comes next depends on what we both do in the lead up to that date.

You see, we both have work to do, Enoch. As i uphold my responsibility of ancestral healing and one who has accepted that this is one expression of my purpose, you too must do your part. I don't know what that is, but imagine it might include navigating uncertain terrain, moving through discomfort of release, living into freedom, doing the work of elevation, summarizing the lessons from your life, and/or much more or different.

Perhaps in time, you may get to know me as i have come to know you through the eyes of your daughters and sister.

Whether you do or not, i am grateful for the relationships i have with them to you. I am grateful for the

---

[16] Nana Esi is a deity in my spiritual order who is an elevated ancestor that serves as an Okyeame (spokesperson) for the deities and helps people transition to the spirit world. She is also known for addressing many issues involving families, women, children and more.

sense of belonging they offer through our evolving relationships and their memories of you.

Travel well,
      Ife

Spirit of the Wind, carry me
Spirit of the Wind, carry me home
Spirit of the Wind, carry me home to myself
- Brooke Medicine Eagle song excerpt

A Letter to Unknown Native/Indigenous American Elders

Dear Elders,

I saw you. Or perhaps some of you in my dream this morning. I remember being in a large open room filled with people of all ages, many of whom were people Native/Indigenous to this land mass named the United States. I sat at the edge of a beautiful woven cloth on the floor (as was the arrangement throughout the room; different groups of people/families sitting around fabric), deep turquoise with beautiful patterns that included red and white. On it were bowls of food, such as rice, corn, fruit, and other prepared delights. There were also flowers. It felt like a festive and jovial time.

To my far left, the door opened and in walks a group of women dressed in white blouses and turquoise skirts, similar in color to the cloth under me. Stoic and serious they were as they slowly entered the room and looked around, eventually pausing in my direction. The energy that accompanied them swirled around the room. It found and encircled me. I began to cry suddenly and without warning. I bawled harder than i ever have before in my life. Between breaths i tried to talk. I wanted to tell those around me why i was crying but couldn't get the words out. I didn't feel sadness, rather pure emotion and an unexplained sense of connection. I was so moved by their presence. I knew they came for me.

The woman i was sitting with, a round faced Native/Indigenous woman with long Black hair pulled back, picked up something i made. It was a square mat with two round sticks affixed to opposite sides. On top of it were two small bowls of grains and water and a few other items. By the time she lifted it up, i too was standing and the ladies who entered the room had approached us. The one in the front reached into the red leather pouch hanging from her neck and pulled out a small handful of red sparkling dust that she sprinkled in the center of the mat. The woman holding the mat then handed it to me in the tradition of gift-giving we seemed to share: she motioned to place it into my hands three times, the third time gently placing it in my hands and letting go.

During this blessing, i began to awaken. My ankle was throbbing, making me aware that i was dreaming. I wanted to stay so i could take in more of the scene and have a lasting memory of the entire experience, even understand more of what was happening between the ladies and myself. But the growing pain in my ankle woke me up.

As i was returning to my body, something inside of me knew it was you all who paid me a visit to show or tell me something. Though i still want to sit with the experience to peel back the layers of meaning, one message was clear: you are real and in my life. I want you to know that i see you, that i acknowledge you, and that i sit in gratitude for your blessing in the dream and for your presence in my life.

You must have known in these series of letters to my ancestors, i hadn't planned on writing one to you all explicitly. To me, you were among my *unknown* Nananom, or elevated ancestors, mainly because i didn't really know who you were or what to call you. There also hasn't been a clear recollection of you all by family members who i've known in my lifetime. The two tests i've taken so far revealed scant evidence of Native/Indigenous American DNA in my blood. I didn't want to lay claim to you all without concrete evidence or really knowing/feeling you directly in some way.

Still, the way you showed up let me know you are in fact present in my life. Immediately i knew we were connected, if not by blood than certainly by spirit. I remember hearing snippets of stories from people with spiritual sight who told me, *"There is a big Indian man who walks with you."* On multiple occasions, i have been reminded that there are people who take us in and become guardians of sorts through relationships, as opposed to by blood. My granddaddy and i are not blood relatives, but we are bound by the strength of the connection we shared in life. My dad's family and i are not blood related, as i recently discovered, but we are nonetheless connected in important ways.

Indeed, it was not unheard of for Native/Indigenous communities on this land mass to take in Black/African people on the run from the brutal conditions of the enslavement system. In some communities, we found love, created families with and took care of one another in the midst of colonization, enslavement, murder, rape and theft.

Also, we were not always so kind to one another. History has shown there were those among us who brutalized, killed and enslaved one another. This should not be glossed over or forgotten, as history has a way of repeating itself if we don't heal wounds, repair relationships and cultivate a shared understanding of our Oneness. This relational work is necessary alongside the strategizing, planning, and precipitating system changes that honor life and our sacred relationship with the earth.

The women who visited me reminded me that whether we share blood or not, our ancestral connections are expressed in past relationships, shared histories and the winds, waters and lands that are our relatives. We took a powerful journey together most recently along the Mississippi River, where we—along with many Black and Native/Indigenous women who participated in this pilgrimage—offered prayers of healing for ourselves, our relationships, the waters and lands that hold us all. As water walkers, we joined a deep healing process that began long before us and will continue long after.

The living spirits who showed themselves to me and blessed me in my dream gave me something. I am curious; what shall we do together next?

In anticipation,
    Your spirit child

messages travel through myriad corridors weaving
millennial cycles of genetic memories
severed by tragedies but not
out of reach for
the seers

Letters to the Most Ancient Ones

Dear Abusua Panyin,[17]

It is with great humility and reverence that i write this letter. I come before you as a child would approach a respected elder in the community; one who has amassed tremendous wisdom over the years through myriad trials and tribulations, hard work, generosity and demonstrated love for family and community. With open hands and heart i come with questions, thirsty for any morsel of wisdom, advice, and answers you would be willing to peel off and pass my way.

How could conversations with other ancestors take place without seeking your guidance and wisdom? You who lived and died (perhaps multiple times) several millennia before my soul made its journey here? So many of my immediate questions have been directed toward my most recent ancestors; those within the past five to seven generations whom i've been privileged to learn more about in the past year and a half thanks to conversations with my

---

[17] The eldest ancestors

mom, aunts and recently discovered relatives, as well as sleuthing on ancestry.com and other places. The beauty of this work has been to hear and speak the names of those whom we collectively remember, to be able to call their names during libation and honor their names in other ways.

But i want to reach back further, to you whose names i don't know. You who lived in a time before the waves of European followed by Arab followed by European invaders pillaged the lands of my ancestors on the African continent, extracted our knowledge and enslaved our people over the past 2,500 years. I want to go back even further before the masses were ruled by a small elite of dynastic kings to a moment in history where families and communities lived and worked in cooperative and reciprocal relationship with one another and the environments of which they were a part. I want to connect with you, Ancient Ones, who can provide insight into and keys for understanding who we were when we were free.

What was it like to live together in ways that were shared, communal, reciprocal and regenerative? How do i get to know you and learn about your greatest hopes and fears? How can i access the wisdoms you passed from one generation to the next through the systems of communication and writing you developed over millennia?

The blood that moves through my veins flows from many origins and one origin. The various tributaries that its lineages have flowed into gave rise to populations who've both benefited from and been harmed by wars, pillaging, enslavement, colonization, elite rule, and more. While i can't in this lifetime turn the hands of time to change the flow of history and the role my ancestors have played on both sides, i can soberly assess their roles in history and identify lessons that can provide guidance for how to live my life now and contribute to the development of community that contains the best of what can be learned.

Within my body runs the blood of creators and destroyers, but it is my spirit that has chosen to be on the side of creation and fight the perpetrators and guardians of destruction. What, then, can you teach me about the work of creation, you who have known that which existed before conditions of hierarchical, centralized oppressive rule of a minority over the majority, regardless of the race, class, gender, generation, culture, and ethnicity of the rulers?

The mere thought of what i might learn from you inspires me to delve into the stories and concepts born within pre-dynastic Kemet over 5,000 years ago. Stories that have largely been destroyed and what survived has been re-purposed for many thousands of years. Of the surviving narratives and documents, many have been translated by Greeks and became the basis of their philosophies, leading to the erasure of their African origins. Of the surviving narratives, many have been transliterated then translated by European thieves who never considered the possibility of literate Black African societies were possible, let alone were more than mere savages awaiting the leadership and direction of

Europeans. Some of the tools they created are useful to beginners of the study of hieroglyphics, but serious work that leads to meaningful conclusions comes from painstaking work of African intellectuals who respect Black life and Black civilization.

Was it you who drew my attention to the Ancient Egyptian Philosophy course at Howard University that would unlock something stored deep within my memories? The material of our ancients was carefully curated by Prof. Gbadegesin, whose approach clearly demonstrated deep respect for the foundations this Black African civilization laid for the world. And though much of the content took place within the dynastic periods, a door was opened. It wouldn't be until much later when i would come to understand the source of the nagging feeling in my gut i experienced when reading and hearing about the rule of the masses by a small elite group of people. These kings, queens, and administrative classes, which are often regarded as evidence of progress over seemingly and previously disorganized societies, are actually indicators of a society in decay. What happens to the spirits, lives and livelihoods of a people subjugated to serve the interests of a small ruling class?

You showed me not only was it possible to live in communal, reciprocal and regenerative relationship with other humans and the environment, but that it was done before for thousands of years before centralized power emerged. And what we now often consider the height of Ancient Egyptian civilization—the dynastic periods—

reframed, actually represent the deterioration of African civilization. The early dynastic period represented a shift from shared leadership to centralized rule, from collaboration to subjugation, from shared labor and community benefit of the fruits of labor to the exploitation of labor of people by a few and the few benefits from the fruits of labor. These human hierarchies and the hierarchies in nature they've imposed are intensely divisive, isolating, and violent in their implications.

But what can this mean, what does this mean in a world and in a moment in history that thrives, values, and perpetuates such a harmful organization of societies? Indeed, throughout the world corporate and world leaders, along with their military apparatuses and mercenaries, impose their destructive ideology and rule over the masses in ways that inspire hunger for the power and wealth they hold. But this begs the question, why should living well be available to a proportionately small group of people at the expense of many living beings and the ecosystems that provide the conditions for their lives?

So much is upside down in this world. And somewhere in it all, your lives and legacies remind me that we can live in right relationship with the earth and with one another. But how?

With Love,
    Afriye

*The Elders tried to
tell us, but
we were too stubborn
to listen*

Dear Abusua Panyin,

I don't know you, but you live within me. It feels as though there have been times that i have lived among you. Can you tell me when my soul was born? After multiple reentries in and out of this world, is there any way to know? Is there any way to peel back the layers of who i am, who i have been, and from where i hail? And what from my many journeys can be carried forward to aid in the work of creation, which to me involves living and working in sacred relationships with others to be in right relationship with other beings?

If you are watching any of what is happening in this world from where you are, you would see that much is out of balance. For example, technological innovation has been touted as a benefit or hallmark of the human race. However, the advancements are driven by profit, which are necessarily destructive not regenerative. Can they even be called advancements? What are we advancing toward if we become more separate from one another? If we destroy our home (this planet) and connections with one another? If the masses are subjugated, oppressed, and exploited for the benefit of a few? If life is made easier for one group because a class of that group has found a way to destroy land, displace people to dig up minerals for use in machines/equipment that a small group can buy, is this advancement?

Why am i writing all of this to you? Though the heaviness of these issues is on my mind and in my body, at the core, i want to connect with you and to let you know that i am concerned about a future for the life on this planet and the role that a small group of humans, with the support of a broader class of supporters, have played in creating conditions so hostile that the future of us all is threatened. In remembering how you lived (through the beautiful work that a group of African intellectuals working together to translate ancient writings you've left behind), i am certain that there is much you can offer in the way of solutions.

I am writing to call upon you to bring forward the principles you embraced into this present moment, at a time when they are needed and when more are open to hear. We are in a time of awakening on this planet. Those of you who are willing to speak to the minds and hearts of your living descendants, please do. There is so much that can be learned from the ways that you lived and worked in cooperative, reciprocal and principled relationships, in life-giving, regenerative, multi-species communities. These lifeways hold within themselves solutions to the myriad crises we face.

After millennium, humans have explored and experimented with various forms of living on this earth and in relation with other beings. And what has increasingly dominated the world over the past 600+ years is not working. The destroyers have had their chance. Let us put an end to this mess.

With Love,
 Afriye

Reflection Space

Please grab your journal and reflect on the questions, thoughts, words, word sequences and/or images that come to your mind as you reflect on the content of this chapter.

I offer the following prompts to get you started, if needed: What themes resonate and why? Have you noticed any thought forms or practices being passed from one generation to the next? What might healing across generation look like for you?

Chapter Six: Conversations With The Mothers Earth and Their Children

Wind Warrior Prayer I

spirits of the wind, *direct with clear purpose and intention this energy within that i may contribute in meaningful ways to the transformation of society.*

spirits of the water, *fill me, feed me, nurture me throughout this journey, let me know thirst so that i can taste water, let me feel hunger that i may learn to eat, let me face death that i may discover life.*

spirits of the fire, *purify my mind, heart, soul and sword, that i may walk fearlessly, with courage, integrity, truth and wisdom, never forgetting my charge, always remembering my purpose.*

spirits of the earth, *root me in the ancient wisdoms and teachings of All My Relations, past and present, seen and unseen, that i may humbly appreciate my place in history, learn from what i've been bequeathed by the ancestors and boldly manifest my destiny.*

light beings and elevated ancestors *help me to gain hindsight, insight, foresight, wisdom and understanding that i may know when, how, what, why and where to do, to be, to show up, to step back, to sit down, to fight, to burn down, to build up, to sum up, to delegate, to pause, to stop.*

as i ask for all these things, i honor and give thanks to those who've come before me, those who stand alongside me and those yet to come.[18]

Dear Mothers Earth,

I want to write a letter to you, Mother, but how is this possible, as you are many and one at the same time? In my mind, you are this ancient living mass of rock, waters and energy that has for millions of years created, sustained, and transmuted life in, into, from many forms. You are a living, thriving, multi-organism that exists within each and all of your creations, ensuring that even at the molecular level our connectedness with you and with one another would be embedded within and embodied by our DNA. How humbling it is to remember that i, and other homo sapiens sapien, are not only related genetically to all living beings, but also to all living beings that have ever existed on this planet.

You've given birth to many billions of species across time and space and yet you are so much more than the sum of them, of us, combined. You created the conditions for some of your earliest offspring to experiment with different chemical combinations. Through trial and error, explosions and successes, primitive life in the form of viruses and bacteria were formed. From them other life sprang and you with them gave rise to an atmosphere that in turn inspired new forms

---

[18] Written by author for one of the gatherings scheduled during the Sacred Water's Pilgrimage, Summer 2020.

to emerge.

But more than an ancient being of rocks, waters, and energy, you are the concentric circles of atmosphere that surround you and the powerful forces of movement inside of you. And still more, you are host to unseen and undiscovered worlds of beings who've managed to avoid the peering eyes and destructive reach of humans. You host portals to other worlds, facilitating the movement of spiritual and ancestral energies from one place to another. Indeed, the living beings that humans have been able to know through our senses and observe scientifically represent only a small portion of who and what you support.

Your relationship with other celestial bodies is curious. The energy that draws you to the sun, that keeps you in its path has scientifically been described as gravity. But it is a pull not of your origin or choosing, rather it is this Grandfather who has tethered you to him. The dynamic relationship you have with one another has made possible all the transformation you experienced since your birth.

You have precipitated conditions that led to massive extinctions and rebirths. You've observed and absorbed many times over the decaying carcasses of your children, powerfully transmuting them into other life forms.

In the course of evolution a species emerged that since the 13 century has held the name "humans." I am curious about the human species, its role and purpose. I am curious about the relationship between us—humans and you, humans and our relatives, your other offspring. Us. I use this word in reference to the species of which I am a part, but it feels awkward. The differences in the spirit of various human populations are so stark at times.

At what point did survival necessitate a destructive imbalance in relationships with other humans and with the environment? At what point did humans consider themselves above everyone else such that subjugation and colonization would be the default relationship? But it wasn't all humans that found comfort in destroying others.

Why is it that populations who lived in balanced relationship with their plant and animal relatives were eliminated and destroyers allowed to thrive so virulently? I understand political history and material realities that positioned some populations over others—spears can't compete with guns. But i am curious if this is what humans do, if left up to their own devices, why do we continue to exist? To eliminate all other species? To poison waters for money and power? To make it so that only a few privileged humans can access clean water, while most have no access or have to pay? To subjugate and enslave species, assign a profit value where possible and eliminate all the rest?

If humans were an experiment, might we have been a failed one?

Curiously,
    Your Daughter

> *the anger is righteous*
> *but we are told to behave by*
> *those who destroy and*
> *we are persecuted by*
> *their systems of destruction*
> *what a mess this is*

Dear Mothers Earth,

I struggle at times with the cynicism that comes from having lived on this earth for over fifty years. The hope, possibility, and revolutionary fervor that i felt and embodied in many ways as a younger adult has shifted as destructive ideologies, policies and practices have become normalized, seeded within each generation, reinforced in schools, and embedded in daily life, even as there are informal or implied rules about who can benefit and who cannot. Violence is a way of being that is considered normal, even desirable if it generates profits for members of the ruling race-class-gender-culture, as it does, for example, with domestic and global militarism, in video games, and legal frameworks that protect wealthy people who harm others through corporate malfeasance. But opposition to violence in the form of protest by people who have been harmed is criminalized.

My heart has become a bit hard over the years witnessing decades, generations of destruction, thousands of years of ideologies and cultural practices that are based on scarcity, hoarding, theft, and destruction. I am angry at the millions of innocent children who are taken advantage of, raped, sold, forced to work, abused by adults that don't have regard for their own lives, let alone others. I am angry at the conditions that created people who feel or have been so harmed, isolated, alienated by their families, societal systems, that they would in turn harm others.

I am angry that Black people can't catch a break anywhere in the world, that virtually everywhere we are, there is an external force, facilitated by internal ones, dealing crushing blows at our attempts at self-determination. I am angry at the anti-Black racism embodied not only by the ruling race-class-gender-culture, but also by some Black people and other people of color who fail to recognize that our liberation is tied up with one another. I am angry that after hundreds of years in modern history, Black people are treated as though we can't be angry about what has happened to us in history and must instead suck it up, hold it in, and turn the other cheek. Angry that little girls and boys who've been abused by degenerate adults can't receive the protection required for them to be, to feel whole.

I am angry at the wanton killing of trees, pollution of lands, air, and waters for profit-driven development, industrialism, and raw material extraction. I am angry and sad that capitalists have fought to ensure that companies have rights but have fought to deny the rights of Mother Nature. I am sad that we have grown so dependent on industrial produced products and foods that we've forgotten how to meet our own needs, while becoming complicit in supporting energy intensive, harmful practices that produce unsustainable amounts of waste and pollution and facilitate mistreatment of workers.

I want you, Mothers, to bring balance into these unbalanced relationships. I want you to send hurricanes through wall street, to swallow all the cancer alleys and the people who run and operate them, i want you to elevate the many examples of aboriginal peoples around the world who know how to live in right relationship with you so that we all can remember how this is done. I want you to teach humans who embody hierarchies that this way of being in relationship is problematic. But you can only do what you can do.

I want to be more hopeful. But when i look around at the people, the levels of brutality in history, the evolving dependence on industrial produced goods over time, the continued push for single-use products, throwaway goods and sacrifice zones and people, it all just makes it so hard for me to imagine a way out of this tangled mess. There are populations that not just benefit from the harm and destruction of people, communities, species the world over, but who also build out entire systems and empires to perpetuate and profit from such destruction.

Sometimes hope is hard to hold, hard to come by.

Frustrated,
    Your Daughter

Yemaya

*in form and substance
you are mysterious as
you are familiar*

Dear Sacred Waters,

Perhaps a letter to you now is appropriate and necessary to cool the temperatures rising in my body and ease the feelings of inadequacy that arise in the face of seemingly overwhelming odds. Temperatures that increase when i think about the ways that humans have been so unjust to one another and all our relations, seen and unseen. If the form you take in this moment are tears that draw out the anger that lives in my heart, the frustrations and embarrassment of the ways i've been complicit in reproducing harm, i thank you for your graciousness and ask for support in turning feelings into actions. If the form you take in this moment are the abundant rains pouring from the clouds above, thank you for the heaviness you clear, the life you give and the cycles of birth-death-rebirth you support.

    You are among many healers and teachers who've offered key lessons at pivotal moments. So many i recall come from times in life where you've showed up in one or more of many forms and expressions. In 2000, it was in the form of the ocean.

    I was seated on the hot sands of Labadi Beach in Ghana, making prayers to you in the form of the Atlantic

Ocean. How powerful and humbling it was to be there. What words do i have to describe what i saw, what i felt? Allow me to go back as if i were there.

I am sitting on the dry sand, a short distance from the edge of the water's reach, wrapped in a beautiful piece of African fabric. The sand is hot, yet comforting like a warm, weighted blanket. I plunge my hands beneath the surface to absorb the heat until the temperature equalizes and then i do it again, in another spot.

In front of me, as far as i can see, the waters are vast, expansive and ever moving, holding memories and secrets and lives. I wonder what they've seen, what stories they hold, even though i've concluded that i know the answers already: history told me what happened here many years ago. I feel a sharp pain in my belly at the thought of what happened. Yet sitting here, hands in sand, i fixate on the sun's dance on the water's surface, in rhythmic alignment with the waves' rise and fall.

It was from here and many places like this that many of my ancestors were forcibly stolen from their lands, homes, families, and communities and imprisoned in death fortresses until it came time to transport them to the Caribbean and Americas. My heart is heavy as i pray, imagining the emotional, physical, psychological, and spiritual torture and suffering that millions endured over many cycles of capture and transport: women, men and youth torn from their homes, the pain of never seeing their loved ones, the fear of not knowing what lay ahead, the searing tears of metal against flesh, utter disregard for life, not able to protect one another or themselves, the powerlessness felt. Oh, my heart aches. The spirits of the innocent bodies who landed in your sacred waters i pray for their peace and elevation. I pray that you hold their spirits and remember their lives, preserve their memories so their lives would not have been in vain and transmute their fear and rage into forms that would serve as warnings for the world's descendants.

Sitting on these hot sands, you in the form of tears pour from my eyes as i remember all these things happening. I see them in my mind's eye. Although i wasn't here 400 years ago and i don't know what happened firsthand, somewhere within my body a memory surfaced. A young girl, crying, wrists bound, dragged from a holding cell, standing in the very spot i sat in, looking at the waters with fear, trepidation, and anxiety, before being loaded onto a boat. There were others.

As my prayers come to a close, i hear the laughter and calls of my spiritual family to join them in the water and enjoy our time together. I wipe my eyes and breathe deeply, slowly rising and walking to meet my sister Fofie in the shallow waters just before me. As i approach her, i see that she is in a similar heart space as i look in her eyes; we offer one another a comforting embrace. We quietly walk together further out, allowing the heaviness of what happened here just a few generations ago to give way to gratitude for the privilege of being here as a descendent who has returned. Together, hands clasped, we immersed ourselves completely underwater to wash away not the memory, but the sadness we held around it so that we could open ourselves to experience the beauty of this place. We take a few breaths together and then begin to share water dreams with one another as we slowly waded further out. Though we were able to touch the ground beneath us, we both treaded water to allow us to talk with greater ease.

After about 30 minutes or so, we decide to head back to the beach and join the others, but somehow are unable to move. Instead of going toward the beach, we are slowly being pulled further out by a deceptively strong undercurrent. We glance at one another with fear-filled eyes as it becomes apparent how serious of a situation we are in. *Odomonkuma, Nana Asuo Gyebi, Nana Adade Kofi, Nana Sankofa, oh Nsamanfo, help us get back to shore,* we pray as we proceed to swim with all our might.

I see Nia's face, her big brown eyes and radiant smile. I hear her 7 year old laugh as i make a funny face at her and she tells me i am silly. What is she doing right now in this moment? Is she thinking of me? If i don't make it back will she remember me? If i don't make it, what will happen to her? What will her life be like? Who will give her what only i can uniquely give? Who will tell her about periods and changing bodies and boys or girls? Who will teach her how to swim? I thought about how her birth and very existence saved my life, gave me a reason to live and in moments when i wanted to leave it all behind, she reminded me that if for no other reason, i am here to make sure she has a life. My heart pounds harder as i resolve that i must survive this, i cannot give up, i have to be there for every part of her life. I look over at my sister, catch her eyes and say at the same time, as though we are in one another's heads, *we can do this.*

I steady my breath so that i don't panic and tear into the water with all the strength and focus i have: my arms paddling, my legs kicking, every muscle called upon in this fight for my life. *Catch, power, recover, catch, power, recover, breathe,* i repeat over and over again with Nia's face in my mind. I am not advancing at first. *Catch, power, recover, catch power, recover, breathe*, i continue and eventually i begin to move. After what feels like forever, we break free of the undertow, thrusting into a faster pace. My body soon brushes against the sand beneath me and i crawl as far i can until i collapse in exhaustion. Adrenaline still rushing through my body, i lay there, shaking in fear, breathing in relief and offering prayers of gratitude.

Why after all of the prayers and affirmations and gratitude did you, sacred waters of the ocean, want to take my life? I asked this question many times. Many times i am reminded that we all are who we are; you are who you are. We are beings composed of matter and energy or spirit, guided by purpose (forces, instinct), with an essence (nature, personality) that makes us who we are. We all have a purpose. Your purpose in that moment was to draw out to the deeper waters anyone or thing caught in the undertow. In that moment, my will had to be stronger than yours for me to live.

I wonder if that lesson needed to be revisited over a fifteen years later when my sister Fofie and i visited a different ocean. This time the Pacific. The year was 2016 and i had garnered enough courage to leave my home and visit Fofie for a month or more (if i could make it happen). I visited with the purpose of supporting her at a time in her life when she needed it. But if i were to be honest with myself, the visit came at a time when i myself needed support. Perhaps you knew. Perhaps you knew the heaviness i felt in my spirit at that time. Years of struggle with sadness, unhappiness, self-doubts, unworthiness. Years of living in unhealthy relationship with myself and others. Years of internalizing anger, loneliness, traumas, and more. It felt as though my soul didn't want to be here anymore, but maybe instead, it knew that i needed help.

    Fofie and i stood on the sand together, taking in the cool air, listening to your waters slap against the boulders just to our right, watching the birds alight on the waves in search of food. The waves looked pretty strong coming in, so i took my time to identify the safest place to lean over, water bucket in hand, to gather water. When i found that place, i made offerings and prayers and stated my intentions before climbing up and then down the large rocks to a place that seemed untouched by rushing waves. Just as i lowered the bucket, a wave blindsided me, knocked me off the rocks and into your waters, reprising memories of the earlier experience and triggering fears. Though it could've been completely coincidental, it felt deeply personal.

    When you knocked me into the water and tugged at my feet, as though you were trying to carry me further into you, i saw a choice before me: i could leave and return to the waters with you, joining my sea relatives, which might have provided a welcome escape from my life; or i could continue living. Perhaps the lesson wasn't that extreme. I held onto the rock until the wasters receded a bit and slowly pulled myself out. It took forever for me to fill the water containers because i was so unnerved, shaking, wondering why.

What was it i was to learn?

Interested,
    Your Kin

Guide Me Assase Yaa

The journey long
The path elusive
Today i am blind
Moving with trust, Dear Mothers

I don't know where this journey will lead
Except that it is
In the direction of greater
Freedom

Mothers
Make light my journey
I lay my troubles down
At the foot of the Great Tree
Embrace me as i am
And we become one
(June 2018)

Dear Assase Yaa, the Mothers Earth,

I guess within you exists all things. Good people and bad. Those committed to destroy for personal gain and those generators and defenders of life. But wherein lay the balance when a small group of well-armed people wield tremendous power over the masses? How to bring things into balance when the systems—political, economic, social—are designed to keep many asleep, recruit defenders of the destroyers? Perhaps these aren't questions that are appropriate for you to answer. As a member of the species who is responsible for these levels of destruction, these are questions to explore with others of like minds and hearts.

Given where we are in this historical moment, a question for us to ask and answer in thought and deed is how all humans live in a healthy, responsible and generative relationship with you and with all of your children such that the depletion of natural resources is avoided, biospheres are healthy and future generations of all life forms have a chance to thrive. When i say all humans, i don't mean those with the monetary resources or wealth are the ones who get the privilege to live in healthy relationship with the earth or that sustainability ought to be governed by the whims of capitalism, an extractive economic system that by its nature is unsustainable.

Rather i mean how can we all live—and importantly how can we all *want* to live—in a responsible, healthy, and regenerative relationship with you and your children? This includes—and i need to say this explicitly so it doesn't get lost—it means Black and Black Indigenous people around the world, it means First Nations people that are indigenous to this land mass (Turtle Island), Latine, people of Asian descent and many other people of color, poor folks, elderly, gay/lesbian, trans and gender non-conforming, disabled, etc. *What does a non-hierarchical, post capitalist society look like?*

What i mean when i write that we live in right relationship with the earth, with nature and with other life forms, is that we as humans see ourselves as a species that doesn't lord over other species, but rather lives in community with them, in a reciprocal relationship where we return in equal measure what we take from the environment and where we don't take from nature more than is necessary for the system to naturally recover from the loss.

I think about how we move humans can do this by first recognizing that we CAN, in spite of the fact that shit is bad and will continue to get worse for a while. Indeed, for many people it is already bad and worsening. But that we can, and we should, do something about it. In so doing, we must learn from the past and in the process, we need to take care of one another.

Seriously,
    Your Daughter

Oh Mothers!
How indescribable my love
for you and your children.
How deep the gratitude
for what you make possible:
the life and lessons, communities and relations,
balance and cycles.
May i honor the sacred place
i hold among your children
who are my kin
plant and animal, human and ancestral,
seen and unseen.

Dear Assase Yaa, the Mothers Earth,

It was from a woman that i grew up feeling as though she never liked me, a person who rejected me, that gave me an opportunity to connect with nature. During the few visits, i recall at my paternal grandmother's house, i was given the space to roam freely in the woods and build lasting relationships with the plant and tree relatives that lived together in community in those woods long ago. Deeply impressed in my memory are the fragrant woody scents that filled the misty air early in the morning, the light crunch of fallen leaves as i made my way to the fallen tree that was sometimes my science lab and at other times a horse or a bed. I remember the buoyancy of the understory and the feeling of being seen by all the tree beings. It was there that i freely explored mosses and insect colonies on fallow logs, talked with and listened to the trees and exchanged breaths with the plants. I felt seen, held, welcomed, and protected.

One of the Elders of that place visited me in a dream last year; one whom i call Grandfather Oak. I saw myself laying on my back next to it. Before I knew what was happening, Grandfather leaned over and placed its crown in my abdomen, sending waves of its medicine through my body. The experience was unexpected, shocking, unbelievable, and it lasted just a few seconds. Almost as quickly as it appeared, it was gone. I woke up feeling deeply touched by the generosity of the visit and opportunity to remember. The blessing to re-member.

You, Mothers Earth, speak to us constantly and in so many ways. Through your internal processes. Through your children. Often the subtle messages from seemingly benign encounters contain the most prolific lessons.

In 1996 I attended women's sun dance in Arizona, in the desert outside Flagstaff. There I was, with sisters, to lend support to women whose life circumstances, spiritual callings, heart desires led them to engage in what traditionally and historically has been a place for Lakota men to offer something to their family and community. Between dances, i walked off to sit quietly under the sun and listen. To still my heart-mind-spirit and be open to whatever may or may not come. Determined to have a spiritual experience, I sat with eyes closed trying to quiet my mind. Sipping water, wiping sweat, attempting to listen intently. After what felt like a long time I opened my eyes.

A voice from the sky didn't speak to me. No divine messages appeared in my mind's eye. I resigned myself to simply absorbing as much sun as I could and receiving its energetic rays. The land was vast and open. The ground appeared dry and still.

In repositioning myself to maximize the sun's kiss on my body, my eyes landed on a quite unexpected scene. Where upon first glance it looked as though little life existed, endless communities of ants were busily moving in and out of tunnels, transporting food, dragging grass bits and communicating in languages I had no access to. The thoughts emptied from my mind as I watched with great interest. Their level of coordination was astounding. Each dedicated to completing its specific task within a larger community or species aim. What might that be? I cannot say. A surface interpretation from a human outsider might simply say to feed the queen, to ensure that the larvae are provided for, to contribute to the community into which it was born and for which it will ultimately die.

Each ant has a sacred purpose within the broader project of survival. And the queen's honors her purpose by producing the next generation of ants. Within the context of my conversations with you, where i am exploring purpose beyond my family lines, what is it that i am realizing, learning, and understanding?

Wondering,
    Your Daughter

Reflection Space

Please grab your journal and reflect on the questions, thoughts, words, word sequences and/or images that come to your mind as you reflect on the content of this chapter.

I offer the following prompts to get you started, if needed: What themes resonate and why? What might life for you and your loved ones look like beyond systems of exploitation and oppression? What do regenerative, restorative, reciprocal, just, and loving relationships look like (feel like, taste like, smell like) – with you, with others, with the natural world, in society? What shifts are needed in society to create or restore such relationships? What shifts are needed inside of you to create or restore such relationships?

Chapter Seven: My Gift to Reader, My Kindred Spirit

When i began writing this book, i set out with a clear intention of re-membering my purpose in life. Spelled in this way, with a hyphen, i acknowledge that i came into the world with something (e.g., a charge, mission, purpose) that during life became lost or forgotten - or both – and set the intention of bringing them into my consciousness. But i also knew that there was another element of purpose: that which i create and re-create, define and redefine over throughout life.

A lot of what i learned throughout life resurfaced in the writing of these letters and was affirmed by the wisdoms of those to whom i was speaking. This was a beautiful dance of noticing and being curious and penning messages as they took shape while they moved from someplace in my body to my mind for translation. I can say i wrote these letters and that would be accurate. Also true is that inspired by my curiosity, members of my body community, ancestors and the natural world engaged with me in this journey of reflection, this exploration into deeper meaning, this search for clarity of purpose. And here are some lessons that emerged.

Working with Self

Lesson 1. Our body community is ground zero, the place

where exploration of who and what we are (in motion, as a verb) begins. I began this part of my journey (seeking meaning and understanding with the aim of re-membering purpose) at ground zero: my body community. This internal conversation of existential meaning of my life, those parts that were held within my being, i explored. This exploration initially took the form of the fast talking, ever questioning, Mind seeking answers from the wise, measured, elder aspect of the body community: the Soul. It is the nature of the mind, to be curious, seek answers and know all the things it can. It is constantly moving, at least in my body community, and often makes things more complicated than what they are. However, in the end, simplicity prevails.

Quite simply, i was reminded that i came into this world and was able to grow into the person i am because a variety of circumstances (internal and external) favored my birth, growth and development. Simply being born and fulfilling a commitment, in practice, to wake up each morning, make it through the day, go to bed and night and wake up the next day to do it all over again meets an important part of my life purpose; that part that i brought into the world. Pretty basic, huh?

Given the narratives i created in my mind over the years rooted in ideas of worthlessness and unworthiness, this wasn't a simple process for me. Arriving at this point, i had to wade through years of accumulated negative self-talk that weaseled its way into the fabric of my sense of self, that place beyond habit. So, digging into the root of these negative narratives, deconstructing them and healing or evolving them is some of the work i continue to this day. And importantly, this ongoing work is one way i am leaning into my purpose because it actively removes unhealthy thoughts, which are damaging to the body community.

The process of removing negative thoughts and their corresponding practices (i.e., lack of self-care, staying in unhealthy relationships, causing self-harm in various ways, etc.) opens the way for and requires the abundant seeding of positive, healthy, and nourishing ones. Abundance is important here because more of this goodness is needed to fill the spaces left by years of unhealthy thoughts and practices, heal the conditions that allowed them to stay so long, and address the ghosts of these old thought forms that are certain to arise from time to time going forward.

Lesson 2. Personal experiences account for so much of this internal messaging around self-worth, but it is important to understand that they take place within broader historical processes wherein human populations have constructed and evolved entire systems and relationships through violence, intimidation, theft, and exploitation. The ideologies and cultures reflected in these systems, as well as their corresponding policies and practices, value white bodies over Black ones; wealthy and middle-class people and communities over working, poor and non-classed people; cis-gendered male bodies over female and transgendered ones; adults over elders and children; people of the global north over people of the global south. The list continues. All of this shows up in the systems of this society, including education, housing, banking and finance, law, criminal justice and more. They also show up in social relations of production which is defined as "people's relationship to one another (individually and collectively), to the land, to the means of production, and to others engaged in production."[19]

Having been born and raised in the United States, i was—as many are—forced fed in school a diet of historical lies written by descendants of the colonizing enslavers turned industrial capitalists and philanthropists. A child, no different than millions in this country, forced to navigate the impact of these lies on the self-worth of my family and community, the apparent limited possibilities of life, love and relationships, how we regarded, spoke to and treated one another. Growing up as a poor Black girl in the Midwest, i was taught that my people had nothing of value to offer the world beyond entertainment, specifically music and sports. This impacted how i engaged with and understood the circumstances of my life, which made me question the value of my existence and my purpose in life over and over again.

Creativity flows freest when it's rooted in

---

[19] Sullivan, T. (May 2002) African-American Women and Production: A descriptive analysis of the shifting roles of Black women in the process of production, 1972-1999. (Unpublished doctoral dissertation). Howard University, Washington, DC.

> confident knowledge of oneself, of one's personal narrative, and of one's ancestral history. The obverse is equally true: Children who get taught, by implication or by explication, that no one like them ever created anything, grow up intellectually fragile, psychologically diffident, easily shattered in the face of hostile challenges, especially if those challenges come from the same culture these growing children have been trained to look up to for inspiration.[20]

Having this internal conversation between my mind and my soul, wherein i reflected on various experiences and observations, led me to situate these experiences within a broader context. I realize that part of the work of discovering and creating meaning and purpose within this world is to free my body community as best as i can from the impacts and constraints of colonization and the colonized mindset.

This has been, and continues to be, quite an undertaking, as i've been under the influence of systems of settler colonialism, enslavement, and colonial capitalism for generations. Ideologies of supremacy, hierarchies, separation, individualism, commodification of living systems and nature, domination, exploitation, etc. are accepted and considered to be the norm within society. Therefore, extricating myself the grip of these ideologies

---

[20] Armah, *wat nt shemsw: Myth, history, philosophy and literature.* Per Ankh Press (2018), p 15.

and what they look like in my particular set of realities is a substantial body of work i continue to this day.

I've been able to work through quite a few things, like learning about the complex histories of Black people around the world and releasing judgment about what was and was not possible in other times and places. For example, i often wondered why in various periods of European and Arab invasions into Africa we didn't stop them from taking our lands, brutalizing and subjugating our people, and crippling our development? I grew up feeling at times as though i was on a losing team. And when introduced to traditional African spirituality, i wondered the same things about the deities. How did they let this happen? How did they let innocent children, boys and girls, be violated so systematically and brutally? Whew…this is so hard to write. These were questions that even then i was embarrassed to ask because the answers, to the extent that they can be extrapolated them from oral and written history, reveal hard truths about our complicity in these historical processes, as much as they invisibilize African people's organized and coordinated efforts to fight back.

This work of disrupting colonial influences has assumed many forms. For example, taking charge of my own learning by learning with others in study groups, listening to wisdoms of the elders, reading/studying, reflecting on what i was learning and journaling about it all was incredibly transformative. Doing this work radically shifted my understanding of history and the role of my people in it and helped me to understand a bit more the nuances and complexities they faced. Similarly, i have been able to appreciate my place—and that of my generation—in the continued flow of history and ask what is the contribution i can make?

Society and systems of education as purveyors of colonial capitalism regard all of nature as a commodity, humans too, which means that any being, body of water, air and land is valuable to the extent that it can be exploited (bought and sold) in the marketplace for profit. So, for me, decolonizing my body community has meant building and deepening relationships with my relatives in the natural world—bodies of water, communities of trees, spirits of plants and more. What this looks like is spending time in nature, greeting the beings in all their forms, paying respect in the form of prayers, small gifts, and learning about the practices that harm nature, while doing what i can to stop them in my own life.

Lesson 3. In this conversation between Mind and Soul, i also was reminded that while there may have been cosmic forces contributing to my existence (who's to say?), a dedicated intellectual (mind-led) pursuit of purpose takes away from being leaning into my life with all my being, taking in each moment and being fully present in each experience. It is not *why* we live, but *how* that is important.

How i live my life is important. And as i move through life, i check in with myself more regularly on some key questions: How am i living? Do my thoughts and deeds align with the core principles and wisdoms held within my body? When i make decisions, am i noticing the affirmations of my heart or the tugs in my gut that suggest alignment or misalignment with core principles? I often think about harm and to what extent a thought, decision or action may cause harm to other beings. Though it is impossible for me to move through this world without causing any harm, i can do my best to try not to and be transparent and accountable when i do.

Lesson 4. I can dedicate my life to looking for, thinking about and focusing on this question of purpose in places outside of myself. But doing this and seeking acceptance from others because i didn't regard my own existence and thoughts as worthy, only keeps me looking. I can't find out there, answers that lay within. My existence is meaningful enough and making the decision to awaken each day leads to its fulfillment.

The mind, in its effort to find or assign meaning to experiences and observations creates ideas, identities and narratives that i become attached to, invested in and emotionally connected with; so much so that they have times taken on lives of their own, becoming the things that i react to, as opposed to reality itself. Experiences of pain, rejection and trauma were interpreted as evidence of my worthlessness. And it was within these moments that i wondered about my purpose. Why was i here, why would i choose to remain if this is what life is meant to be?

It was in these and other difficult moments that i

visited time and time again this question of purpose. Doing so in those moments kept me going because if nothing else came out of the questioning, it was an understanding that i was connected to something bigger than myself. And, as i matured, i learned that i was connected with generations of people who came before me, live as my contemporaries and will come after i am gone. This sacred connection to others across time and space led to the next phase of exploration of my purpose, which was with the ancestors.

Working with the Ancestors

Lesson 5. As the living beings they are - alive in my body community, my heart, spirit, my memories, as well as in the materials (books and otherwise) that hold their stories—the ancestors influenced my journey in unexpected ways. For one, what began as a search for purpose became a journey of discovering what we've done together and exploring what remains to be done collaboratively. This was made possible because of the relationships we have that exist via shared lineage and through conscious cultivation over time. It is this second part—conscious cultivation over time—that builds the relationship by keeping them alive, present and working in my life. Conscious cultivation of relationship with the ancestors begins with acknowledgement and continues with various practices that range from calling their names; making prayers with, for and to them; being curious about and holding conversations with them; making offerings to them; singing songs for them; and much more.

There are many throughout the world that honor the ancestors, keeping them alive in their lives and communities. In my home, i've created a sacred place that i call an ancestor altar. While having an altar is not necessary to deepen relationships and communicate with the ancestors, for me, dedicating a physical space to them makes room in my home for their presence. It is like having an elder in the family live with me that i can greet each day, give water and flowers to, love up on and seek wisdom from. Regardless of what is going on in and around me, this sacred place is where i can quietly sit to center myself and connect with them.

Creating an ancestor altar or space is quite simple and requires intention and focus. There are as diverse examples of ancestor altars as there are people in this world, but building one often begins with cleaning the space, however big or small and clearing the energy through smoke (burning a resin, dried herbs or incense or dried herbs) and/or sweeping the area (branch or special broom) with spiritual bath or holy/blessed water. There are many other ways, but these are a couple. Then cloth is often placed in the area, on top of which images of ancestors are placed or artifacts they owned or that represent them. And then the ongoing ritual and practice is what keeps them alive in and around us. On a regular basis, offer flowers, change water, and make foods that they liked or made from recipes your family has passed down. Both my granny and granddaddy drank coffee, so i place coffee on the altar to honor them. My granny liked a particular powder, so i sometimes sprinkle some in the air. The offerings vary but are nonetheless made on a regular basis.

Lesson 6. It is in these and other practices that the ancestors are kept alive in and around us. And, importantly, it is where generational healing can be facilitated as well. I came to learn that one part of healing and repair work can take place in the quiet of my sacred altar spaces, through prayer, conversations, and various ceremonial practices. For me, another part of this work involves cultivating, evolving, and repairing the relationships with their descendants, my living relatives, as best as i can. And still a third part of this of this work requires breaking unhealthy cycles that pass from one generation to the next.

It has been in the relationships with my daughter and granddaughter, as well as with my newly discovered paternal sisters, aunts, and cousins, that these important ancestral bodies of work have played out. As a young parent who didn't yet realize the ways that trauma and arrogance showed up in my life and impacted others, i made decisions and mistakes that cultivated dynamics within the relationship between my daughter and me that gave rise to distance and tensions as she moved into and through puberty and her teen years. Implementing practices with her that broke cycles of abuse and harm required intentional work and practice over time, much of it taking place during her twenties and my forties, when we both were able to do this together.

Her parenting with her daughter and my daughtering with my mother, and all the learning, healing, and growth that we are experiencing in conscious and subconscious ways is forging a more whole and resilient link between the ancestors who've come before us and those who have yet to be born. Our work together is not without mistakes, nor have we exhausted and explored all possibilities together. But we do the best we can, given who we are and the nature of our relationships. What does this look like? With my daughter, this looks like having honest sometimes difficult conversations, each sharing our perspectives, listening to one another with love, admitting mistakes and refraining from judgment. It is apologizing. Yes, apologizing to my daughter for mistakes i made and forgiving myself for making them. With my mother, this looks like being curious about her thoughts and her life, taking interest in who she is as a human being and stepping back when it feels as though i am going to far.

Working with Others

The guidance provided by the ancestors seamlessly led me to explore and interrogate ideas about being human and my identity as a human being; the only species in history as we know it to be responsible for such levels of destruction that the existence of all life on the planet is threatened. The clarity and reassuring calm provided by the ancestors quickly transmuted within my body when engaging with the Mothers Earth to what felt like anger, frustration, hopelessness and overwhelm as my mind was flooded with images of unspeakable abuse, exploitation and violence at the hands of a relatively small group of people seeking and holding onto their definitions of militarily imposed power and profit. This makes me remember something my mom used to say, "the world is going to hell in a handbasket" and i've wondered if this is the case, why does purpose matter? Why do all this hard work of waking up each day, living in alignment with principles and engaging in ancestral healing when no matter what i do, oppressive, militarized, and well-funded generational forces continue their destructive frenzies on populations, lands, waters and other forms of life that have been made vulnerable by their policies and practices?

Lesson 7. Change is constant. This is a lesson as terrifying as it is satisfying: terrifying because the entire existence of the human species[21] and all life as we know it is threatened because of human's harmful practices within only the past 250'ish years; and satisfying in that we have a chance to turn this ship around by becoming, embodying solutions to the crises we face as individuals, communities and beyond.

Internally, for me this has involved the deliberate, painstaking and often challenging work of decolonizing,

---

[21] The entire span of human life, roughly 200,000 years, is a mere grain of sand in the life of the earth, which is over 3 billion years and counting.

detoxifying, and healing my body community, while learning and experiencing joy, wellness, love, and growth in new ways. I am a work in progress but committed to identifying the thought forms and practices that require decolonization and detox on a regular basis and replacing or letting them go. This includes reducing my consumption overall and reliance on plastics and items in disposable containers. It means cutting back on addictive substances, including sugar, coffee, television, social media, and other things that dull my mind and/or senses and keep me reliant on industries that cause harm to people and the planet. It looks like learning how to grow food, reducing reliance on fossil fuels and building relationships with the communities of trees and other forms of life in my area. It means being kind and loving, having patience and drawing healthy boundaries.

With others, this valuable lesson on change reminds me of the importance of humans working together to heal the impacts of the harm we've done to one another and the earth, repair the relationships that have been damaged through the harm and evolve our ways (practices, beliefs, how we show up in the world, etc.) as a species to reduce future harms. In other words, be the change, embody the change that the world needs in community with other like-minded, like-hearted people moving in the same direction.

In the end, and ultimately, the question for purpose brought me to a place of remembering: re-membering the hidden messages of purpose in my body community that affirm the intrinsic value of life in all its forms and the importance of living in principled relationship with all forms of life, which include the ancestors.

> So, "What is the purpose?" This question arises because you have not experienced the grandeur of existence. You have not experienced the magnificent nature of your being. That is why you are asking, "What is the purpose? What should I do to make this life meaningful?" You don't have to do anything. If you could sit here for one moment and experience this, you would know you don't have to do anything. Just being alive is grand enough.[22]

---

[22] Sadguru, "What is the purpose of life?"
https://isha.sadhguru.org/us/en/wisdom/article/what-is-the-purpose-of-life

Reflection Space

Please grab your journal and reflect on the questions, thoughts, words, word sequences and/or images that come to your mind as you reflect on the content of this chapter.

      I offer the following prompts to get you started, if needed: What themes resonate and why? What lessons does your life offer? What does your life suggest about your purpose? What do your experiences say about the things your soul came to learn in this lifetime?

Afterword

Dear Daughter,

You inspired this body of work. But more than this, you inspired a process of healing through writing, writing for healing. It was that day in the kitchen, early 2020 when i shared that something was inside of me that needed to be born, and until i gave birth to it, i wouldn't be able to do other things that called me. *What should i write? What would you want to read?* Your response was shocking in its content and simplicity, *I want to read about you.*

I felt humbled and honored that you would want to learn about my life, and perhaps learn something from it. In the course of writing, i noticed that insecurities and moments of shame around circumstances that i had not yet dealt with arise inside of me. I felt embarrassment about some of the decisions i'd made and their impact on you. I noticed the judgment still i held toward myself after all of these years. How exhausting!

Oh, my dear daughter, i remembered the many times when i simply didn't want to live. And though i've expressed gratitude to you, your spirit, for saving my life, giving me reason to live, i've never discussed some of the circumstances surrounding those moments. More than that, i realized that i hadn't released the shame and judgment that accompanied the experiences leading to those moments.

Yet, there you were again, blessing me with your

sacred medicine. There was something in that moment of you expressing an interest in my life that gave me permission to explore where this might go.

As i sat down to pen the first letter between my mind and soul, i began a journey of surfacing things that my body has held onto for so long: lingering insecurities, feelings of unworthiness, doubts, not thinking i am smart enough or good enough or thin enough or anything enough. Though i had done a lot of work over the years, and in particular over the past few years, to heal, there were some old things that lingered, like the stuff that i never wanted to face because it was too hard or because i felt that by now, i should have been dealt with them.

These lingering feelings over time grew into communities of unhealthy energies and thought patterns that nurtured habits and unhealthy physiological responses. Serious excavation was needed. This journey provided the opportunity to really dig in deep.

In the end, i leaned into the discomfort. I opened my heart and spirit to a level of vulnerability that at times was cringeworthy. It's not just the traumatic moments and how i responded that left me feeling embarrassed, which to be clear weren't the whole of my life, but even the questions i asked and have been curious about are kind of odd, i think. For much of my life, instead of embracing my uniqueness (which i've learned is not so unique) i tried so hard to be something else. I understand that part of this comes from feeling rejected by part of my family at such a young age. But the point i am making is that i tried to fit into other people's stories with a fierce willingness to adapt and become someone i think they might like more. And oh, Daughter, i found myself being embarrassed about telling you all of these things. But healing and becoming whole is facilitated by deep honesty with oneself first. And, since you asked, with you.

Because all of life is connected, because my thoughts, behaviors and how i show up in the world is connected with all other life forms, i want to share this journey of discovery and healing with you, your daughter, and others in the event that it may speak to the hearts and spirits of others with similar questions. As i offer this body of work to you, i offer it to others for whom it might provide loving guidance and support.

I thank you.

Love,
    Mom

Resources for Support

Phone Hotlines (24|7 Support)

Mental Health
- **National Suicide Prevention Lifeline:** 988.
    - Military veterans suicide hotline (1-800-273-talk) [press 1]
    - Suicide hotline in Spanish (1-800-273-talk) [press 2]
- **BlackLine:** 1-800-604-5841. BlackLine provides a space for peer support, counseling, witnessing and affirming the lived experiences to folxs who are most impacted by systematic oppression with an LGBTQ+ Black femme lens.
- **LGBT National Hotline:** 1-888-843-4564. The Lesbian, Gay, Bisexual and Transgender National Hotline is for all ages.
- **The Trevor Project:** 1-866-488-7386 or text TREVOR to 1-202-304-1200. The Trevor Project is the world's largest suicide prevention and crisis intervention organization for lesbian, gay, bisexual, transgender, queer, and questioning (LGBTQ) young people.
- **Trans Lifeline:** 1-877-565-8860. This resource is divested from the police. Trans Lifeline is a peer support service run by trans people, for trans and questioning callers.
- **Substance Abuse and Mental Health Services**

Administration (SAMHSA) Treatment Referral Hotline: 1-877-726-4727. For individuals and families facing mental health challenges and/or substance use disorders.
- **National Alliance on Mental Health (NAMI) Helpline:** 1-800-950-6264. The NAMI HelpLine can be reached Monday through Friday, 10am - 10pm ET. The NAMI HelpLine is a free, nationwide peer-support service providing information, resource referrals and support to people living with a mental health condition, their family members and caregivers, mental health providers and the public.
- **Steve Fund:** TEXT STEVE to 741741.

Reproductive Health and Abortion Support
- **National Abortion Hotline:** 1-800-772-9100. Monday - Friday, 8 am - 7 pm EST.
- **Reprocare Healthline:** (833) 226-7821. Call or text between 9am-9pm PT 7 days a week.
- **Exhale Pro Voice** (https://exhaleprovoice.org/): 617-749-2948 (us & Canada) (U.S. Pacific Time). Weekdays 3 p.m. – 9 p.m.; Saturdays 1 p.m. – 9 p.m.; Sundays 3 p.m. – 7 p.m. The textline is also available to partners, parents, family members, friends, and allies – including mental health clinicians, abortion providers, doulas, and others offering abortion-related care.
- **Connect & Breathe:** 1-866-647-1764. Talkline is

open Mon. 7-10pm, Tues., Wed., Thurs. 6-9pm ET and Sat 12-3pm ET.

Resources for People Considering Suicide
- **It Gets Better:** https://itgetsbetter.org/. The It Gets Better Project's mission is to uplift, empower, and connect lesbian, gay, bisexual, transgender, and queer (LGBTQ+) youth around the globe. Also, https://itgetsbetter.org/get-help/.
- **Stop Soldier Suicide**: https://stopsoldiersuicide.org/get-help. This is a veteran-led site aimed at current and former military. There is also a hotline: (844) 317-1136.
- **Accredited Schools Online:** https://www.accreditedschoolsonline.org/resources/suicide-prevention/. Resources are aimed at parents and caregivers with a focus on supporting high school/college students.
- **American Foundation for Suicide Prevention:** https://afsp.org/im-having-thoughts-of-suicide
- **Veterans Crisis Line (run through the VA):** at www.veteranscrisisline.net. Dial 800-273-8255 and press 1.
- **Crisis Text Line**: crisistextline.org text TALK to 741741 to text with a trained crisis counselor for free, 24/7.

Mental Health Resources
- **National Suicide Prevention Lifeline:** Dial 988.

https://988lifeline.org/
- **National Alliance on Mental Illness:** Provides resources about mental illness. https://www.nami.org/Home
- **NAMI Family-to-Family:** https://www.nami.org/Support-Education/Mental-Health-Education/NAMI-Family-to-Family

Mental Health Resources for Black People and People of Color
- **Lifeline Black Mental Health:** https://988lifeline.org/help-yourself/Black-mental-health/
- **Association of Black Psychologists Self-Care ToolKit:** https://www.abpsi.org/pdf/FamilyCommunitySelfCareToolKit.pdf
- **Black Emotional and Mental Health Collective (BEAM):** https://www.beam.community/
- **Black Virtual Wellness Directory:** https://wellness.beam.community/
- **Black Mental Health Alliance:** https://Blackmentalhealth.com/
    - Connect with a therapist: https://Blackmentalhealth.com/connect-with-a-therapist/
    - Listing of psychiatrists https://Blackmentalhealth.co

m/Black-psychiatrists/?wpbdp_view=all_listings
- **Black Women's Health Imperative:** https://bwhi.org/
- **Emotional Emancipation Circles:** https://communityhealingnet.org/emotional-emancipation-circle/
- **Ourselves Black:** https://ourselvesBlack.com/
- **Therapy for Black Girls:** https://therapyforBlackgirls.com/
- **The Safe Place App**: A mental health app for apple and android
- **The National Queer and Trans Therapists of Color Network (NQTTCN):** https://nqttcn.com/en/community-resources/
- **Darkness Rising Project:** https://darknessrisingproject.org/
- **REBUILD (formerly incarcerated BIPOC people):** https://darknessrisingproject.org/help-me-find-a-therapist/
- **Sharing Hope:** https://www.nami.org/Support-Education/Mental-Health-Education/NAMI-Sharing-Hope-Mental-Wellness-in-the-Black-Community. A three-part video series that explores the journey of mental wellness in Black communities.
- **Steve Fund:** https://www.stevefund.org/ is dedicated to supporting the mental health and emotional well-being of young people of color.

Therapy funds/free therapy/searchable directories
- When searching for a culturally competent therapist, try the following directories:
    - Association of Black Psychologists
    - Inclusive Therapists
    - LGBTQ Psychotherapists of Color
    - National Queer and Trans Therapists of Color Network
    - Psychology Today Directory of African American Therapists
- **Melanin and Mental Health**: https://www.melaninandmentalhealth.com/.
- **Loveland Therapy Fund:** https://thelovelandfoundation.org/therapy-fund/
- **The AAKOMA Project:** https://aakomaproject.org/programs/.
- **Therapy for Black Men:** https://therapyforBlackmen.org/therapists/
- **Boris L. Henson Foundation:** https://borislhensonfoundation.org/resource-guide/1653927288609-422c565a-8587.

Additional Therapy Resources
- https://www.Blackgirlssmile.org/resources
- https://www.goodgoodgood.co/articles/Black-mental-health-resources-apps
- https://www.self.com/story/Black-mental-health-

resources
- https://www.verywellmind.com/mental-health-resources-for-the-Black-community-5181656
- https://www.Blackswandiaries.com/resources
- https://theeverygirl.com/online-mental-health-resources-for-Black-women/
- https://www.tricitymhs.org/get-involved/news/357-minority-mental-health-month-resources

Resources and Support for People Seeking Abortion Support

- **The National Network of Abortion Funds:** https://abortionfunds.org/
    - https://abortionfunds.org/how-do-i-find-the-clinic-thats-right-for-me/
    - https://abortionfunds.org/funds/
- **The National Abortion Federation:** https://prochoice.org/
- **The National Abortion Hotline.** https://prochoice.org/patients/national-abortion-hotline/
- **Department of Justice Gender Equality Network:** https://dojgen.org/abortion-resources.

Additional Women's Wellness Resources

- https://www.plancpills.org/
- https://reprocare.com/
- https://www.ineedana.com/

- https://www.reprolegalhelpline.org/
- https://www.abortionfinder.org/.
- https://www.verywellhealth.com/helpful-abortion-care-resources-5649884.

www.ingramcontent.com/pod-product-compliance
Lightning Source LLC
Chambersburg PA
CBHW070147100426
42743CB00013B/2837